CAMBRIDGE LIBRARY COLLECTION

Books of enduring scholarly value

Cambridge

The city of Cambridge received its royal charter in 1201, having already been home to Britons, Romans and Anglo-Saxons for many centuries. Cambridge University was founded soon afterwards and celebrates its octocentenary in 2009. This series explores the history and influence of Cambridge as a centre of science, learning, and discovery, its contributions to national and global politics and culture, and its inevitable controversies and scandals.

A Catalogue of the Egyptian Collection in the Fitzwilliam Museum, Cambridge

Since the first donations of Egyptian artefacts to the Fitzwilliam Museum, including most notably the sarcophagus lid of Rameses III donated in 1823, its ancient Egyptian holdings have grown steadily. This collection, now one of the most important in Britain, was catalogued for the first time by Sir Ernest Alfred Thompson Wallis Budge (1857–1934) of the British Museum's department of antiquities. Budge was a leading authority on ancient Egypt and had himself acquired several pieces for the museum in Egypt in 1886-7. The collection as listed in this 1893 publication included 577 objects: sarcophagi, coffins, canopic jars, mummies, scarabs, sculptures, and other decorative objects. Budge provided transcriptions and translations of the hieroglyphs that appear on the objects with his descriptions of each item. Although the collection has been augmented by many further gifts and purchases, Budge's catalogue remains a valuable record of the collection in the late Victorian period.

A Catalogue of the Egyptian Collection in the Fitzwilliam Museum, Cambridge

Ernest Alfred Wallace Budge

Cambridge
University Press

CAMBRIDGE UNIVERSITY PRESS

Cambridge New York Melbourne Madrid Cape Town Singapore São Paolo Delhi

Published in the United States of America by Cambridge University Press, New York

www.cambridge.org
Information on this title: www.cambridge.org/9781108004398

This edition first published 1893
This digitally printed version 2009

ISBN 978-1-108-00439-8

A CATALOGUE

OF THE

EGYPTIAN COLLECTION

IN THE

FITZWILLIAM MUSEUM.

London: C. J. CLAY and SONS,
CAMBRIDGE UNIVERSITY PRESS WAREHOUSE,
AVE MARIA LANE.

CAMBRIDGE: DEIGHTON, BELL, AND CO.
LEIPZIG: F. A. BROCKHAUS.
NEW YORK: MACMILLAN AND CO.

A CATALOGUE

OF THE

EGYPTIAN COLLECTION

IN THE

FITZWILLIAM MUSEUM

CAMBRIDGE

BY

E. A. WALLIS BUDGE, LITT. D., F.S.A.,

ACTING ASSISTANT KEEPER IN THE DEPARTMENT OF EGYPTIAN AND ASSYRIAN ANTIQUITIES, BRITISH MUSEUM.

CAMBRIDGE

AT THE UNIVERSITY PRESS

1893

Cambridge
PRINTED BY C. J. CLAY, M.A. AND SONS
AT THE UNIVERSITY PRESS
from plates prepared by
MESSRS HARRISON & SONS, LONDON.

DEDICATED TO

JOHN PEILE, LITT.D.,

MASTER OF CHRIST'S COLLEGE, CAMBRIDGE.

A MARK OF GRATITUDE AND REGARD.

PREFACE.

THE collection of Egyptian Antiquities in the Fitzwilliam Museum has been formed by donations from Members of the University of Cambridge and others, and by purchases made by the Syndics. The valuable mummy and coffin of Pa-kep, presented by H. R. H. the Prince of Wales, the granite cover of the Sarcophagus of Rameses III., by Belzoni, the granite sarcophagus of Hunefer, a scribe, by Messrs Hanbury and Waddington, and the coffins of Nesi-pa-ur-shefi by Messrs Yorke and Leake of Trinity College, give to this collection, though numerically small, an importance possessed by no other of the same size. During the last six years a considerable number of smaller but typical objects have been added to the collection. In December 1886, the Vice-Chancellor, Dr Swainson, Master of Christ's College, informed me while in Egypt that a sum of £100 had been voted by the University for the purchase of Egyptian antiquities and asked me to expend this money as advantageously as possible. With the permission of Dr Edward A. Bond, C.B., Principal Librarian of the British Museum, I did so, and purchased as large a number of good specimens of classes of objects which I knew to be unrepresented in the collection of the Fitzwilliam Museum as the funds placed at my disposal would allow. These were exhibited at a meeting of the Cambridge Antiquarian Society in May 1887, when I gave some account of them and submitted a list which was afterwards printed in the *Reporter* of May 17, 1887, No. 686. This attempt to fill up gaps in the collection was continued by the Rev. Greville J. Chester, who in 1890 and 1891 presented to the Fitzwilliam

Museum a considerable number of miscellaneous objects which have helped to make the Egyptian collection more representative. The expenditure of a comparatively small sum of money would now make it a valuable instrument for teaching purposes, and as complete as any collection without constant Government support, in the past or present, can hope to be. It is greatly to be hoped that every opportunity of adding typical objects to this collection will be embraced, for the prices paid for good Egyptian antiquities increases yearly by leaps and bounds, and a time must soon come, if, indeed, it has not already arrived, when institutions with limited means which have chiefly to be spent in antiquities other than Egyptian, will be unable to compete against wealthy collectors and *dilettanti*.

The usual plan of inserting long notes and historical and archaeological dissertations among the descriptions of objects in the Catalogue has not been followed, for both Prof. J. H. Middleton and I thought it better to give these in the form of chapters distinct from the Catalogue. These chapters are published in a separate volume by the Cambridge University Press entitled "*The Mummy: Chapters on Egyptian Funereal Archaeology*." The summary of Egyptian history and the list of the cartouches of the principal kings from Mena to Decius, may be of service to those who use both works.

E. A. WALLIS BUDGE.

CONTENTS.

LIST OF THE PRINCIPAL BENEFACTORS TO THE FITZWILLIAM MUSEUM FROM WHOM ADDITIONS TO THE EGYPTIAN COLLECTION HAVE BEEN RECEIVED.

1. HIS ROYAL HIGHNESS THE PRINCE OF WALES.

   Mummy and coffins of Pa-kep, a water carrier at Thebes, about B.C. 500.

2. GIOVANNI BATTISTA BELZONI.

   Granite cover of the sarcophagus of Rameses III., King of Egypt, B.C. 1200.

3. H. B. BRADY, ESQ., F.R.S.

   A wooden sepulchral chest for holding *ushabtiu* figures.

4. THE REV. GREVILLE J. CHESTER, B.A., Oxon.

   A miscellaneous collection of Egyptian antiquities, consisting of beads, amulets, *ushabtiu* figures, and other objects in faïence, scarabs, vases in stone and earthenware, etc., etc.

5. J. WILLIS CLARK, M.A., Trinity College.

   Bronze figure of Isis suckling Horus.

6. DR EDWARD DANIEL CLARKE, Trinity College.

   Inscribed basalt plinth from a statue of Psammetichus, an officer who lived during the reign of Amāsis II., B.C. 550.

7. A. HANBURY, ESQ., and HIS EXCELLENCY M. H. WADDINGTON, B.A., Trinity College.

A granite sarcophagus of Hunefer, a scribe, about B.C. 400.

8. H. H. HARROD, B.A., Peterhouse.

Two porcelain plaques and head of a bronze uræus.

9. WILLIAM MARTIN LEAKE, ESQ., and the RIGHT HON. CHARLES PHILIP YORKE.

Coffins of Nesi-pa-ur-shef, a scribe in the temple of Ȧmen-Rā at Thebes, about B.C. 1500.

10. THE VERY REV. G. PEACOCK, D.D., DEAN OF ELY.

A limestone stele in the shape of a door of a tomb.

11. PROF. W. ROBERTSON SMITH, M.A., LL.D., Christ's College.

A collection of faïence figures, etc.

12. THE HON. GEORGE TOWNSHEND.

A mummy and coffin of an unknown person.

13. HIS EXCELLENCY M. H. WADDINGTON and A. HANBURY, ESQ.

Granite sarcophagus of Hunefer, a scribe, about B.C. 400.

14. THE VERY REV. JAMES WOOD, D.D., DEAN OF ELY.

A limestone pyramidion from Thebes.

15. THE RIGHT HON. CHARLES PHILIP YORKE, and W. MARTIN LEAKE, ESQ.

Coffins of Nesi-pa-ur-Shef, a scribe in the temple of Ȧmen-Rā, at Thebes, about B.C. 1500.

CATALOGUE.

1. Cover[1] of the red granite sarcophagus of Rameses III., King of Egypt, about B.C. 1200.

This object, one of the most important of the Egyptian antiquities in the Fitzwilliam Museum, was presented to the University of Cambridge by Belzoni[2] in 1823. It was brought by him from the tomb of Rameses III., which is situated in the Valley of the Tombs of the Kings, Bibân el-Mulûk, on the western bank of the Nile, opposite to the ancient Thebes. On the cover is a figure of Rameses III. in relief. He wears on his head the usual royal head-dress with an uræus over his forehead. Above the head-dress he wears the disk, feathers, and horns, . The figure of the king is made to represent the god Osiris in the form of a mummy. The arms are crossed over the breast; in the right hand he holds the crook , emblem of dominion, and in the left, the whip or flail, emblem of rule. On one side of the king stands Isis , and on the other Nephthys ; each embraces the king's body.

[1] See Birch, *Antiquarian Communications of the Cambridge Antiquarian Society*, iii. pp. 371–378.

[2] Belzoni was a native of Padua, although his family came originally from Rome. He left Italy in 1800 to visit various parts of Europe, and married soon after 1803. He arrived in Egypt in 1815, having gone there to build machines for irrigating the country. While there he was employed by Mr. Salt, His Britannic Majesty's Consul-General at Cairo, to remove Egyptian antiquities from Thebes to London, and his investigations at Thebes produced good results. He discovered the tomb of Seti I., and brought the magnificent sarcophagus of that king to England, where it was purchased by Sir John Soane for £2000. His excavations in Egypt lasted five years, 1815–1819. He died December 3rd, 1823, at Gato, in the kingdom of Benin, on the West Coast of Africa. For an account of his labours, see *Narrative of the Operations and Discoveries in Egypt and Nubia*, by G. Belzoni, London, 1820.

Between the king and each goddess is a female figure, with raised hands, accompanied by a serpent. The cover is fractured in many places, and it appears that the damage was done to it in ancient times.[1] Owing to these breaks a large portion of the two lines of inscription which run round the edges of the cover is wanting; each line begins at the head of the cover. The more complete line reads:—

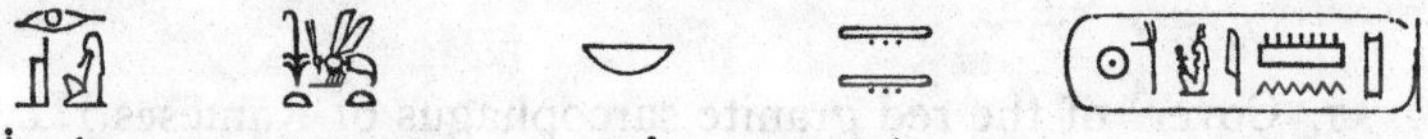

Åusår suten net neb taiu

Osiris, { *King of Upper and Lower Egypt,* } *lord of the two countries,* { *Usr-maāt-Rā meri Åmen* }

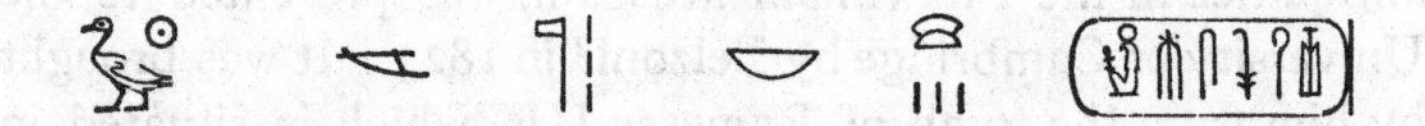

se Rā meri neteru neb χāu Rā-messu ḥeq Ånnu

son of the Sun, beloved of the gods, lord of diadems, { *Rameses, prince of Heliopolis,* }

maātχeru åu-k em neter un - nek em

triumphant! Thou art in the condition of a god, thou shalt arise as

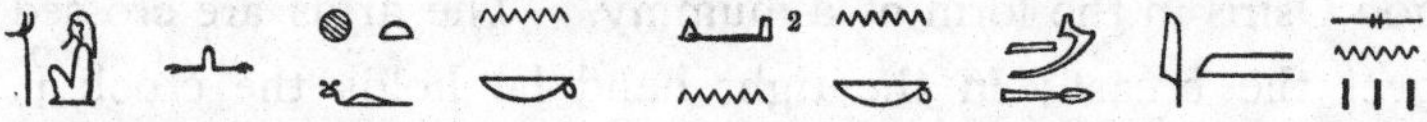

Usr ån χeft nek ṭā-nå nek maātχeru åm sen

Usr, there is no enemy to thee, I give to thee triumph among them,

 . . . . . .

unen - sen em

are they as . . . . . .

The end of the line repeats the names and titles of the king. Of the second line only the first few words giving the prenomen of the king, the name Osiris, etc., remain.

[1] The cover is figured in *Les Principaux Monumens Egyptiens*, par Charles Yorke et M. Martin Leake, Londres, pl. xiv., 1827. On pp. 20–25 of that work is printed a letter by Belzoni to Mr. G. A. Browne, of Trinity College, Cambridge, concerning the inscriptions on this cover.

[2] The cover actually has .

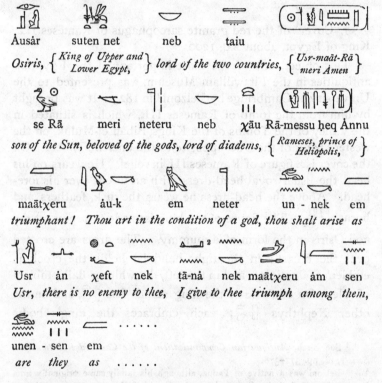

The sarcophagus[1] to which the cover above described belonged, is now preserved in the Museum of the Louvre; it is monolithic, and is in the form of a cartouche ⊂⊃. The inside and outside are covered with scenes and inscriptions of great interest, and relate to the passage of the sun in the underworld; they are selections from the work entitled the "Book of being in the Underworld."

The mummy of Rameses III. was found among the royal mummies brought from Dêr el-Baḥari by MM. Maspero and Brugsch; it is now preserved at Gîzeh. It was wrapped in orange coloured linen and bound round with four bands of ordinary linen. On the outer covering there was no inscription, but round the head was a bandage inscribed with vultures, uræi, etc. It had been deposited in the coffin of Queen Nefert-àri, and was for some time regarded as her mummy; but when it was unrolled on June 1st, 1886, it was seen from the hieratic inscriptions on the bandages that it was certainly the mummy of Rameses III., and that new linen bandages had been wrapped round it in the 9th year of "the chief priest of Àmen-Rā, king of the gods, Pa-net'em I.," about B.C. 1100. M. Maspero has given excellent pictures of the mummy, and of the face and features of the king, and careful measurements of the body and its limbs; his general description of it is as follows:[2] "Les cheveux et la barbe sont ras. Le nez, busqué comme celui de Ramsès II., a été légèrement déprimé par les bandelettes. La bouche est mince; cinq dents seulement sont visibles; la première molaire a été usée ou cassée. Les oreilles sont rondes; le tragus en est peu développé et l'ourlet très fort. Le lobe avait été percé, mais les pendants ont été enlevés dès l'antiquité. Les parties génitales ont été tranchées pour être embaumées à part." (P. 566.)

[1] For a description of it, see *Notice des Monumens exposés dans la Galerie d'antiquités Egyptiennes . . . . au Musée du Louvre*, par E. de Rougé, Paris. 1872, pp. 173–176. "C'est un magnifique monolithe en granit rose, ... d'une largeur proportionnée, creusé pour recevoir la momie royale enfermée dans plusieurs riches cercueils, et couvert de sculptures sur toutes ses surfaces intérieures et extérieures." Champollion-Figeac, *L'Egypte*, p. 348, col. 2.

[2] *Les Momies Royales de Déir el-Baharî*, pp. 563–566.

The tomb of Rameses III., situated in the eastern valley, on the west bank of the Nile, opposite Thebes, is commonly known by the name given to it by Bruce, "the Harper's Tomb." It is one of the most beautiful and interesting of the tombs which now remain. It was originally intended for Set-necht,  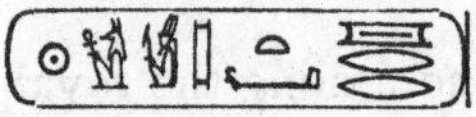, the father of Rameses III., who built the first room only. The sarcophagus stood in a large hall, the roof of which was supported by eight pillars at the end of the tomb. A description of the scenes painted on the walls of the chambers and corridors has been given by Champollion, *Notices*, t. I. pp. 404–424, and 744–752, and by Champollion-Figeac, *Egypte Ancienne*, p. 347, col. 2. The most recent description is by Lefébure, Naville, and Schiaparelli, in *Les Hypogées Royaux de Thèbes*, seconde division, Paris, 1889, pp. 87–120 (*Les Annales du Musée Guimet*).

For a brief notice of the chief events in the reign of this king, see the sketch of Egyptian history at the beginning of this book.

2. Sarcophagus of Hunefer, a Scribe, about B.C. 400.

This grey granite sarcophagus measures 7 ft. 4 in. by 4 ft. by 2 ft. 7 in., and is one of a class of which comparatively few examples remain;[1] it is made in the shape of a mummy. It was presented to the Fitzwilliam Museum by Messrs. Hanbury and Waddington, of Trinity College, Cambridge, in 1835. The outside is decorated with short lines of roughly cut shallow hieroglyphs and figures of the more important gods of the underworld; these were originally painted red to make them more easily seen. The insides of the sarcophagus and cover are uninscribed. The hollow in the sarcophagus in which the mummy was laid is shallow, and the cover is but slightly concave. The edges of both cover and sarcophagus have been damaged in ancient times, and towards the head much injury has been done to the inscriptions either by weather or by rough usage during transport from Egypt.

[1] Compare granite cover No. 78, and a granite sarcophagus No. 18 in the Egyptian Gallery of the British Museum.

The face and features hewn on the cover are of a remarkable character. The ears and nose are large and flat, the lips are thick, and the general appearance of the face recalls to mind the sarcophagi of Eshmûnâzâr[1] and Tabnîth.[2] Under a broad necklace is a figure of Nut with outspread wings, and on each side of her is a figure of Anubis, and an *ut'at*. At the head of the cover is a figure of Nephthys, and a mutilated inscription stating that this goddess has come for the protection of the dead man; and at the foot is a figure of Isis, from each of whose arms hangs *ānχ*, "life," and by each of whose sides is *sa*, "protection." The inscription reads: "Says Isis, the mighty lady, divine mother, 'I have come to thee to protect thee, O Osiris, the *ḥā*, Hunefer.'"[3] The perpendicular line of hieroglyphics reads:—

ȧn	Ȧusȧr	ḥā	Hu - nefer	maāṭχeru	ha
"*Behold*	*Osiris,*	*the ḥā*	*Hunefer,*	*triumphant!*	*Hail,*

mut - ȧ	Nut	pesés	- s	tenḥ	en	ḥer - ȧ . . . . .
mother my	*Nut*	*spreads*	*she*	*wing[s her]*		*over me . . . . .*"

This formula is also found on a granite cover of a sarcophagus of a high official called, Setaa, preserved in the British Museum (Egyptian Gallery, No. 78) On each side of this line are three divisions in which are figures of Ḥāpi, Mesthȧ, Ȧnpu, Ȧpuat, Qebḥsennuf, and Ṭuamāutef. The short lines of inscriptions which accompany each figure begin with *met ȧmaχi*

[1] See *Corpus Inscriptionum Semiticarum*, t. I., pars prima, tab. II., 3 c.

[2] Preserved in the Imperial Ottoman Museum at Constantinople.

[3] 

χer, and contain the name of the god of whom the deceased is a "watchful adorer," and the name of the deceased. The inscription on the right hand edge reads :—

"Says Seb, the prince .... the heir, prince of the underworld, to Osiris, the ḥā Hunefer, Horus, to wit, son of Isis, give to thee the mountains of the underworld their two hands." The corresponding line on the other side of the cover is mutilated.

On the head of the sarcophagus is a figure of Nephthys, with upraised arms, from each of which hangs ☥ *ānχ*, "life." She says, "I come to protect thee, Osiris, superintendent of the house (temple), ḥā Hunefer, triumphant."[2] On the foot are cut , *i.e.*, signs of "protection" and "stability." Around these are inscribed :—

1. 

2. 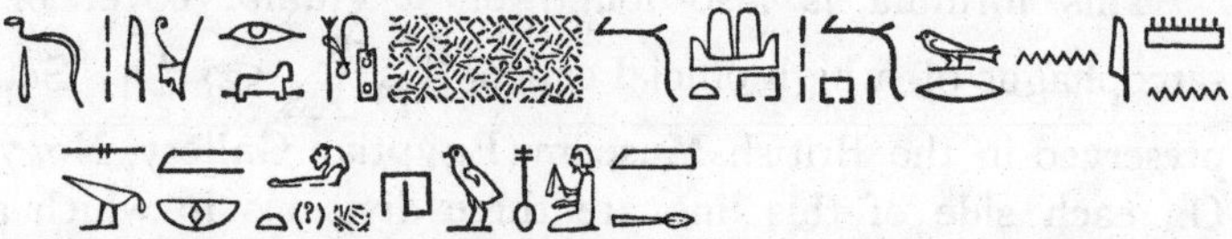

Beginning on the right-hand side at the head, and reading towards the foot of the sarcophagus, are the

[1] Compare cover, No. 78, B.M. 

following deities:—ibis-headed god, Mesthit, Ȧnpu, Qebḥ-sennuf, ibis-headed god, holding , Ḥāpi, Ȧpuat, Ṭuamāutef, and Seb, the "prince of the gods." The lines of inscription relating to these figures are occupied chiefly with the titles of the offices held by the deceased, and the names of gods; they are of little interest.

From the inscription on the foot of the sarcophagus it is clear that the deceased Hunefer was a nobleman of high rank  *ḥā*, and that he held a number of important offices connected with the administration of the revenues of the temple of Ȧmen, and of many other gods. He was "royal scribe,"  *suten nā*, "superintendent of the farms of all the gods," 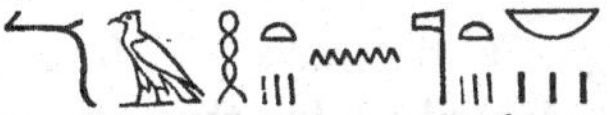 *mer aḥet en neteret nebu*, "superintendent of granaries," 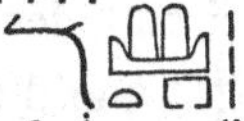 *mer šennet*, "superintendent of the great house of Ȧmen," "superintendent of the treasury of Ȧmen," 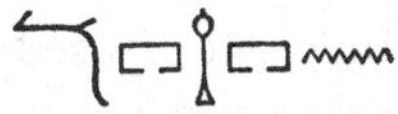 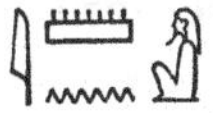 *mer pau ḥet' en Ȧmen*, and "director of the festival of Ȧmen," 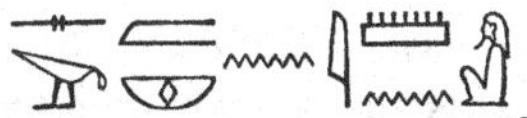 *sem ḥeb en Ȧmen*. The British Museum possesses a beautifully illuminated hieroglyphic papyrus (No. 9901), written for a "superintendent of the king, the lord of the two lands, Men-maāt-Rā (Seti I.), superintendent of the cattle of the lord of the two lands, royal scribe, Hunefer"; but it is not possible that this papyrus and the sarcophagus described above were made for the same person.

3. The Coffins of Nesi-pa-ur-shef, superintendent of the scribes in the Temple of Ȧmen-Rā, at Thebes, about B.C. 1500. Presented to the Fitzwilliam Museum by the Right Hon. Charles Philip Yorke and William Martin Leake, Esq.

I. *The Cover which was laid upon the Mummy.*

(Description of the Outside.)

This wooden cover, which was laid upon the mummy, measures 5 ft. $8\frac{3}{4}$ in. × 18 in., and is made in the shape of a mummied man, with his hands crossed over his breast. The head-dress is painted blue, and over the forehead is a band painted with squares of green and red to imitate inlaid precious stones. The beard is wanting. The hands, which are made of solid pieces of wood, and which were glued to the coffin after it was made, probably once held wooden models of the crook , and whip , which the god Osiris is always represented as holding. On each arm are bracelets, and immediately above the wrist is a figure of the hawk of Horus with a whip on a stand, on the front of which is an uræus wearing the crown of Upper Egypt *ḥeṭ'*. Behind is a winged uræus wearing a disk and having a sceptre , and *ut'at* . Above the hands is a ram-headed, winged beetle having between his forelegs, and the emblems of the circuit described by the sun in the heavens *śen*, stability, *ṭeṭ*, and two uræi between the hind legs. Above the beetle are winged uræi and *ut'ats*. Around the neck is a deep collar, composed of rows of lotus buds and flowers, painted green and red upon a yellow ground, as are all the scenes on the outside of this cover. Over the portion of the collar which falls under each shoulder is the head of the hawk of Horus.

Immediately below the arms is a ram-headed beetle wearing a disk, on each side of which is an uræus; from each neck hang *ānχ us ānχ*, "life, power, life." Beneath the beetle are the emblem of stability *ṭeṭ*, and the figure *ḥeḥ*, "myriads of years," who has *śen*, "the sun's circuit," upon his head, and *ānχ*, "life," hanging from one arm. On the left hand side is a figure of the god Osiris seated upon a throne wearing and holding a *ḥeq* and *χu* in his hands. Before him, standing on , is the soul of the dead man in the form of a human-headed bird , making an offering of incense and flowers. Behind the soul stands the goddess Isis, wife of Osiris, winged, having *Åuset* on her head, and *maāt*, the emblem of law, in her right hand; above her is written *neter āa Åuset ḥent perχeru*, "Great goddess, Isis, mistress of sepulchral meals." On the right hand side is a repetition of this scene, but the goddess there represented standing behind the soul is Nephthys, *Nebt-ḥet*, the sister of Osiris.

Beneath these scenes, and under a star-spangled sky, holding *ānχ* in each hand, is a winged female figure; this figure is the goddess Nut, who is here supposed to cover and protect the dead man with her wings. On each side of her are the usual *śen*, winged uræus, and *ut'at*. To the left of the figure is a jackal god, Anubis *Ȧnpu*, who holds between his paws a sceptre, to which is attached a double *menȧt*. In front of the jackal is a standard, upon the top of which are a disk and plumes. Above it is a legend 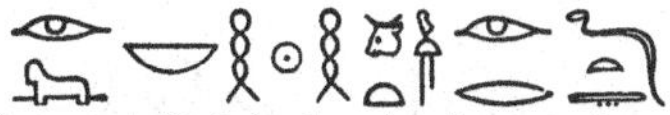 *Ȧusȧr neb ḥeḥ χent Ȧmentet ȧri t'etta*, "Osiris, lord of eternity, president of Ȧmentet, maker of everlasting." The jackal and the standard are repeated on the right hand side, but the legend over the standard reads 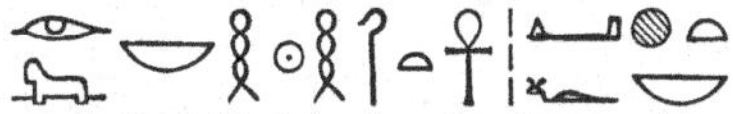 *Ȧusȧr neb ḥeḥ ḥeq ānχiu ṭā-f χet neb*, "Osiris, lord of eternity, ruler of the living; may he grant all things."

The remaining surface of the cover is divided into two halves by means of two perpendicular lines of hieroglyphics, and each half contains five scenes. The hieroglyphics read:—

I. 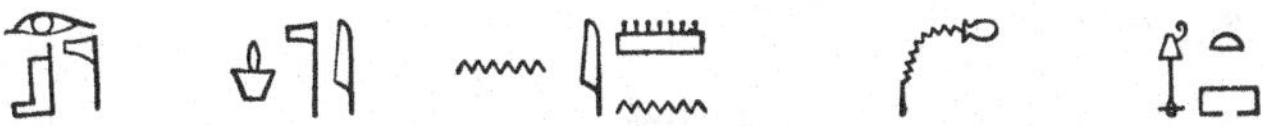

Ȧusȧr	ȧtf neter	en	Ȧmen	āb	ābt
Osiris,	*divine father*	*of*	*Ȧmen,*	*priest of the fine art chamber,*	

ḥer	ān	neter ḥet	en	Ȧmen	pa
president of the scribes[1]		*of the divine house*	*of the*	*Ȧmen*	*temple*

[1] Or "superintendent of the writings."

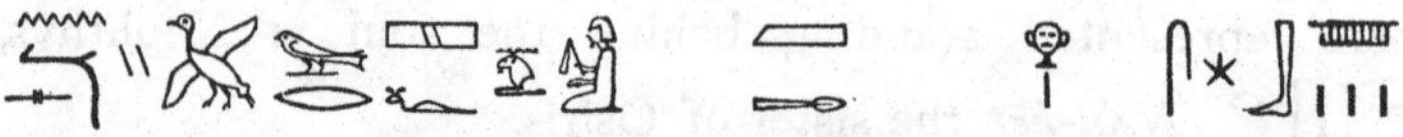

Nesi - pa - ur - śef maātχeru ḥer seb

Nesi - pa - ur - shef, triumphant! Chief of the doors of

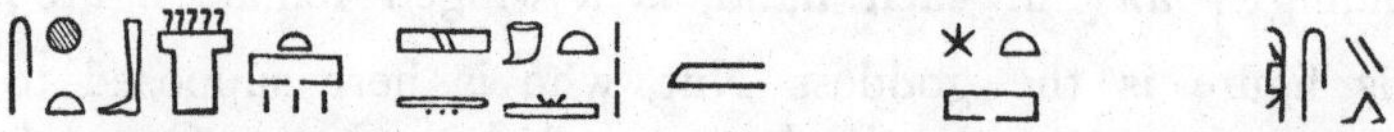

sebeχetet śettat em ṭuat śesi

the pylons hidden in the underworld, follower of

Sekeri en Re-stettet Ȧusȧr em Ṭeṭet ȧri - nef

Seker in Re-stau, and of Osiris in Ṭeṭet. May be made to him

neter sentrȧ qebḥ embaḥ neteru nebu

[*offerings of*] *incense and libations in the presence of the gods all of*

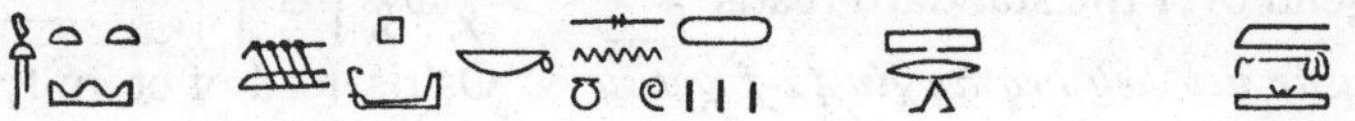

Ȧmentet śesep - k sennu per embaḥ

Ȧmentet! Mayest receive thou cakes, and come forth in the presence of

Ȧmen - Rā

Ȧmen - Rā!

II. 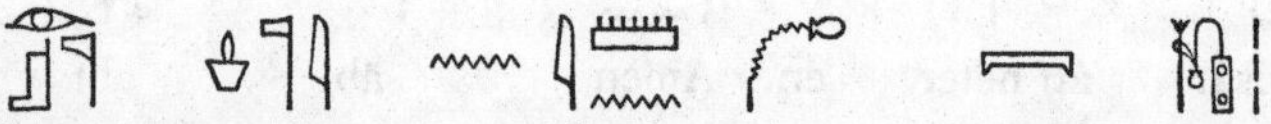

Ȧusȧr ȧtf neter en Ȧmen āb ḥer ān

Osiris, divine father of Ȧmen, priest, president of the scribes[1]

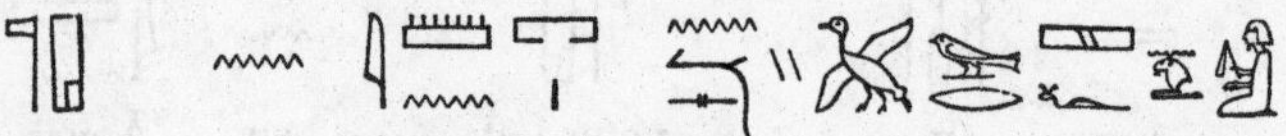

neter ḥet en Ȧmen - pa, Nesi - pa - ur - śef

of the divine house of the Ȧmen temple, Nesi - pa - ur - shef,

[1] Or "superintendent of the writings."

maātχeru em nebt ī em neter-χert per

triumphant, as a lord cometh into the underworld. May come forth

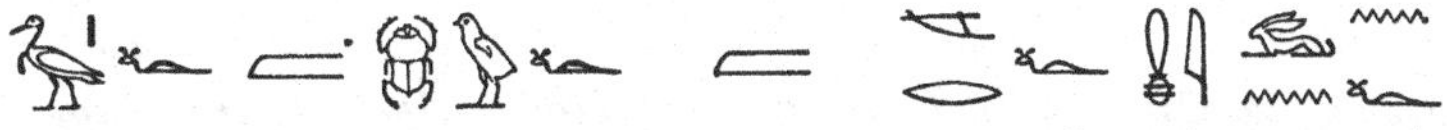

ba - f em χeperu - f em mer - f mā un - nef

soul his in evolution his according to will his, as did he

ṭep ta er maa āten em uben - f

upon earth, to see the Disk (of the sun) in rising his,

Temu em ḥetep - f ṭā - sen nek ḥetep

and Temu[1] *in setting his! May give they to thee offering of*

t'efau ḥer χaut en Un-nefer.

tchefau food upon the table of Un-nefer![2]

The five scenes to the right of this inscription are as follows:—

I. Osiris seated in a shrine, wearing disk and holding  and ; a winged *ut'at* and uræus. Behind him stands "Nephthys the divine sister" 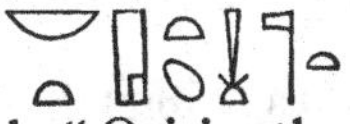 *Nebt-ḥet sent.* Before him stands the deceased, "Osiris, the divine father of Amen, Nesi-Āmen," 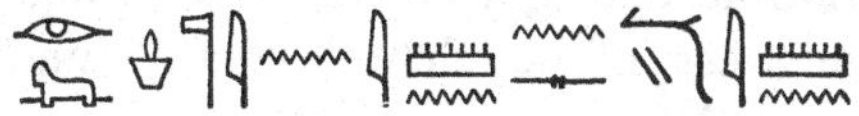

[1] The name of the sun as closer of the day.

[2] A name of Osiris.

Ȧusȧr neter ȧtf en Ȧmen, Nesi-Ȧmen, offering incense. Above the shrine is the inscription :—

ȧmaχ Ȧusȧr neb ḥeḥ χent Ȧmentet sebebi
Homage to Osiris, lord of eternity, at the head of Ȧmentet, traversing

ḥeḥ em āḥā - f ṭā - f ḥetep t'efau
myriads of years during life his ; may give he offerings of t'efau food !

II. The hawk of Horus in a shrine, wearing the crowns of the north and south, standing on a pedestal, from the front of which spring a crowned uræus, a winged *ut'at* and uræus. Behind stands the goddess "Neith, the divine mother"  *Nit neter mut*, having *ānχ* in her right hand and on her left arm. Before the hawk stands Nesi-Ȧmen, bareheaded, offering. Above the shrine is the inscription :—

ȧmaχ Ptaḥ Sekeri Ȧusȧr ḥer ȧb ḥāt ṭā - f
Homage to Ptaḥ - Seker - Osiris, within the shrine. May he give

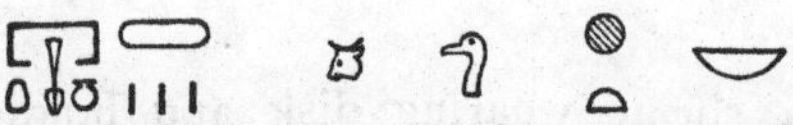

per - χeru ȧḥ apt χet neb
sepulchral meals, oxen, ducks, and things all.

III. Shrine in which stand "Osiris" in the form of a ram-headed god, with horns and uræus, and "Isis, the mistress of sepulchral meals," under the form of a lion-headed goddess. Before these gods stands the deceased with both hands raised in adoration, and above him is the legend  *Ȧusȧr Nesi-Ȧmen em ḥetep*, "Osiris, Nesi-Ȧmen, with an offering." Above the shrine runs :—

ȧmaχ Ḥāpi neter āa mȧ χet neteru tā - f

Homage to Ḥāpi, the great god, ... of the gods. May he give

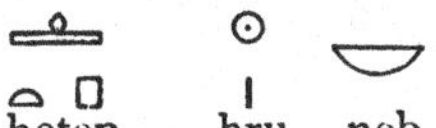

ḥetep hru neb

an offering day every !

IV. Shrine in which stand the two children of Horus, Ḥāpi 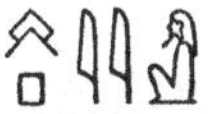 and Qebḥsennuf . In front of these gods, near a table of offerings, is the soul of "Osiris, the divine father of Ȧmen, Nesi-Ȧmen," making an offering of incense. Above the shrine is the inscription :—

ȧmaχ Qebḥ - sennu - f neter āa χent

Homage to Qebḥsennuf, the god great, at the head of

Ȧmentet

the underworld.

V. The goddess Nephthys in a shrine kneeling. Above is the inscription :—

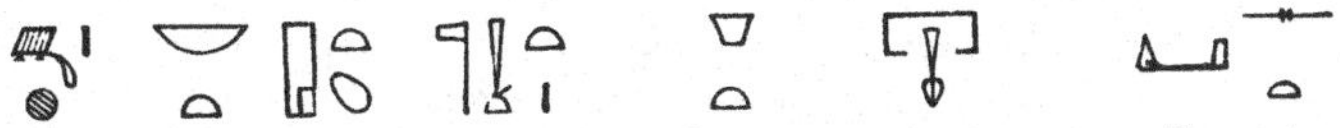

ȧmaχ Nebt - ḥet neter sent ḥent perχeru ṭā - set

Homage to Nephthys, divine sister, mistress of offerings. May she give

triumph !

maātχeru

The five scenes to the left of the inscription are as follows :—

I. Osiris seated in a shrine, dressed as before described, and standing behind him is  *Åuset urt ḥent perχeru*, "Isis, the great lady, mistress of sepulchral meals." Before him stands the deceased offering to the god  and . Above the shrine is the inscription :—

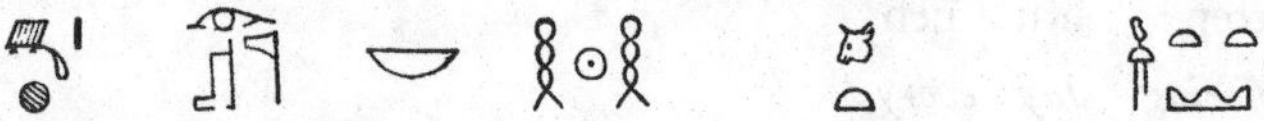

åmaχ Åusår neb ḥeḥ χent Åmentet
Homage to Osiris, lord of eternity, at the head of the underworld,

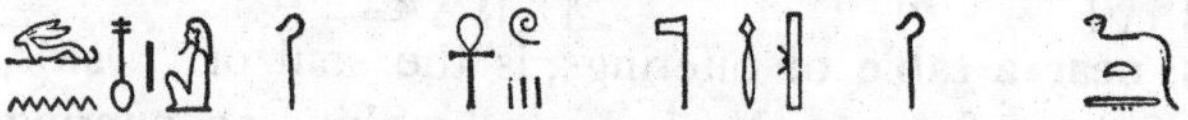

Un-nefer ḥeq ānχiu neter āa ḥeq t'etta
Un-nefer, prince of the living, god great, prince of everlasting.

II. Hawk of Horus in a shrine as before ; behind him stands Nephthys. Before the god stands the deceased bareheaded, offering , a buckle. Above the shrine is the inscription :—

åmaχ Ptaḥ Sekeri Åusår ḥeråb ḥāt ṭā - f χet
Homage to Ptaḥ - Seker - Osiris within the shrine. May give he thing

neb nefer āb χet neb nefer bener
every good, pure, thing every good, pleasant.

III. Shrine in which stand Osiris "prince of Amenta" (the underworld), in the form of a ram-headed god with horns and uræus, and  *Ḥeru neter āa*, "Horus the great god," under the form of a jackal-headed god.

Before these gods stands the deceased offering incense. Above the shrine is the inscription :—

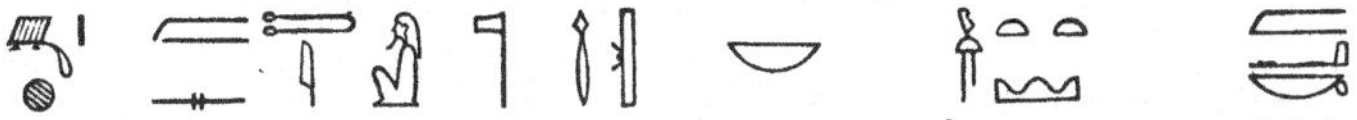

åmaχ Mesthå neter āa neb Åmentet Māk
Homage to Mesthå, god great, lord of the underworld. Verily

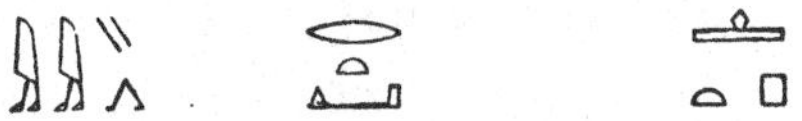

ī er ṭāt ḥetep
come to make an offering.

IV. Shrine in which stand the bearded human-headed child of Horus *Mesθå*, and a jackal-headed god. Before them is the soul of the deceased, "with an incense offering," *em ḥetep*. Above the shrine is the inscription :—

åmaχ Ṭuamāutef neter āa se Åusår ṭā-sen
Homage to Tuamautef, god great, son of Osiris. May grant they

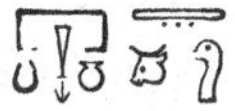

perχeru
sepulchral meals !

V. Shrine in which kneels *Åuset urt neter mut*, "Isis, the great lady, divine mother." Before her are *u'tat* and *neferu*. Above the shrine is the inscription :—

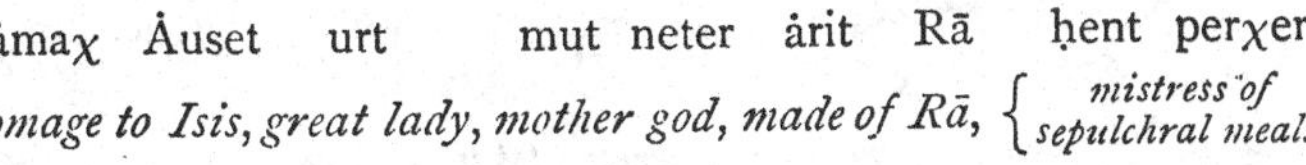

åmaχ Åuset urt mut neter årit Rā ḥent perχeru
Homage to Isis, great lady, mother god, made of Rā, {mistress of sepulchral meals.}

The pillars of each shrine are formed by a placed above a lotus column.

The feet of this cover are wanting.

II. *The Cover which was laid upon the Mummy.*

(Description of the Inside.)

On the inside of this cover the following scenes are painted in yellow upon a purple ground :—

I. The water of the sky, upon which is a boat ; under the boat at each end is a fish; one is called the *àbṭu* fish, , and the other the *àntu*[1] fish . In the boat is a ram-headed beetle, under each wing is a serpent , and between the hind legs is *śen*, emblematic of the sun's course through the heavens. Above is the disk of the sun with uræi .

II. Bent female figure, with hands and feet touching the ground. On the back of this figure, which represents Nut, the goddess of the sky, sails a boat, on the front of which is *ut'at.* In the boat are a beetle, the goddess Maāt , Rā the Sun-god, , and a god who rows the boat with two oars , on the blades of which are painted lotus flowers, and . The heads of the oars, and the posts upon which they rest, are hawk-headed. Behind the god who rows the boat is *śes.* The bent female figure is called *Nut urt mes neteru,* "Nut, the mighty lady, genetrix of the gods,"[2] before and behind her is a winged *ut'at.* Beneath her is the god

[1] The *àbṭu* and the *àntu* fishes are referred to in the XVth chapter of the Book of the Dead. (Naville, Band I., Bl. xiv., ll. 13, 14) [ ] *maa-nà abṭu sep χeperu ṭekai-à ànt em χeperu-s.* "May I see the Àbṭu fish in the season of [his] coming into being, may I see the Ànt fish in his evolutions."

[2] B.M. coffin cover No. 15,659 gives .

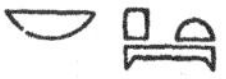 "*Ḥeka ta neter āa neb pet*, Ḥeka . . . . . the great god, lord of heaven," having  on his head. On each side of him is a bird in adoration with human head and hands.

III. Lion, couchant, with bearded human head at each end of his body; on each forehead is an uræus. This lion represents the day, and one head is called  *neter āa nebt ṭuat*, "Great god, lord of the dawn," and the other  *neter āa nebt Ȧment*, "Great god, lord of the west" (*i.e.*,evening). In front of each is a winged uræus. Above is a boat in which is a figure of the sun on the horizon  *χut*, and on the disk is Rā, the Sun-god, having disk and uræus on his head, and the sign for life  *ānχ* in his hands. He is adored on each side by a cynocephalus ape with uplifted hands.

IV. Star-spangled sky on which lies the mummy of the dead man, which is here described as  *Ȧusȧr neb Ȧbṭet*, "Osiris, lord of Abydos." Above are a pair of arms  embracing the disk of the sun , which shines upon the mummy, and whose rays cause five plants to sprirg up from it. The sun is adored on each side by a kneeling ram-headed god with uplifted hands, who is called  *neter āa*, "great god."

V. Shrine or ark, formed by a serpent, in which stand, 1, the goddess Isis, lion-headed, and wearing an uræus: 2, the god Cheperȧ, beetle-headed; and 3, the god Osiris, ram-headed, and wearing an uræus.

There are in the British Museum two covers of coffins (Nos. 15,659 and 22,542), the decoration of which is similar to that of the coffins of Nesi-pa-ur-shef. No. 22,542 is painted on the inside a light purple colour, and is uninscribed; No. 15,659 is painted inside with a colour similar to that of the cover of Nesi-pa-ur-shef, but the arrangement of the scenes is different, both as regards contents and order; they are as follows:—
I. Winged beetle, with disk, in a boat sailing across the sky; at one end of the boat is the *ȧbṭu* fish, at the other is the

àntu fish. II. The goddess Nut with upraised arms, from each of which hangs ; above her 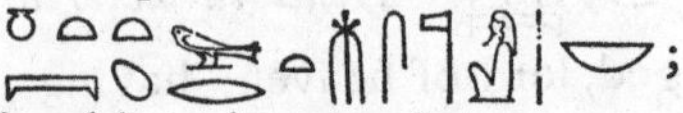; on her right Osiris, on her left Anubis; she stands on . Below is inscribed, "Osiris, lady of the house, singing woman of Àmen, Ta-sau-t-necht. Says she, 'Hail mother Nut, spread [thy] two wings over me,'" 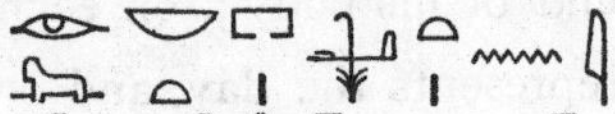

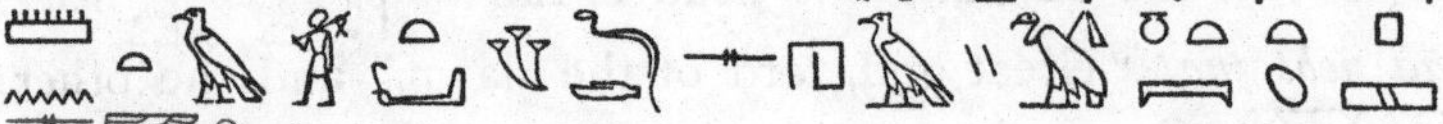

 *Àusàr nebt pa qemāt en Àmen Ta-sau-t neχt t'eṭ-s hai mut Nut peśeset tenḥ ḥer-à.* III. To the left of this inscription is written:—

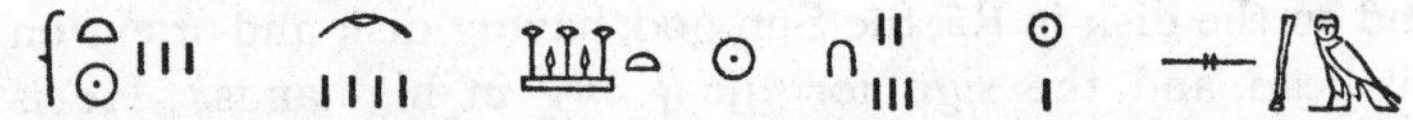

r enpit emt àbeṭ fṭu śet hru met'-ṭua hru senem

Year three, month four of sowing, day fifteen, the day { *f making a second time* }

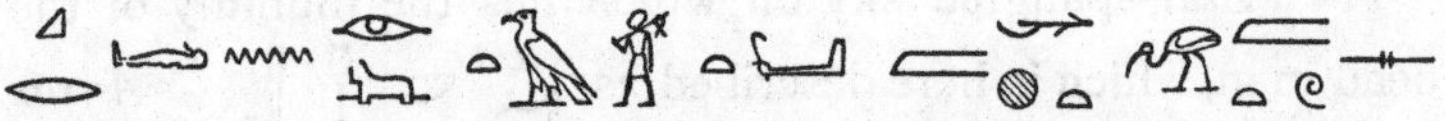

qeres en Àusàr Ta-sau (?) t-necht emχet qemtu - s

the burial of Osiris, Ta-sau (?) t-Necht. After was found she

àu θeti nai mesu χer nau

carried away the children of the cemetery the

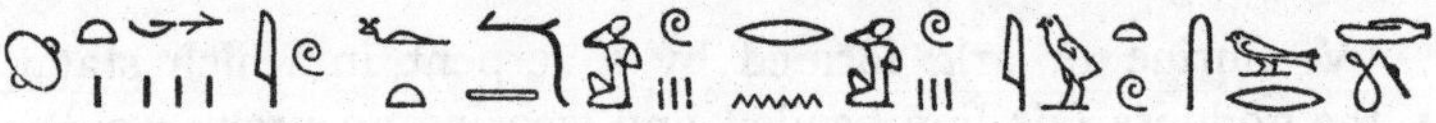

ut àu fetta - u ren-u àutu s - urṭ

coffins were blotted out names their; one made grow

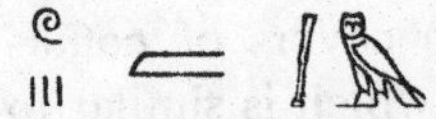

u em nem.

them a second time.

III. *The Inner Coffin of Nesi-pa-ur-shef.*

(Description of the Outside. The Cover.)

The head-dress is painted blue, and over the forehead is a band painted in squares of red and green, with yellow borders, to imitate the inlaying of precious stones. The face is painted yellow, the eyebrows green, the nostrils are hollow; the beard is wanting. The arms are crossed over the breast, and the hands, one of which is wanting, originally held models of the and , which the god Osiris, in whose form the coffin is made, is always represented as holding. A deep collar of five rows of lotus buds, flowers, etc., painted red and green upon a yellow ground, falls over the breast; the part of it which lies over each shoulder is ornamented with a head of the hawk of Horus. Above the arms are the figure of a ram-headed beetle wearing a disk, *ḥeḥ*, "millions of years," winged uræi and *ut'ats*. The wrists and arms are ornamented with bracelets, and on each arm is a scene in which the deceased is represented lying on a bier , by which stand Isis and Nephthys weeping and lamenting for the dead. Beneath one bier are the four "Canopic jars," all human-headed (*sic*), in which the intestines of the deceased are preserved; under the other bier are two *only*, together with uræus , *ānχ* and . Above each arm is the god Osiris seated in a shrine, wearing the *atef* crown and holding in his hands and ; before him is the soul of the deceased, with both hands raised in adoration.

Below the arms are two scenes:—

I. Ram-headed winged beetle, emblematic of Rā and Cheperȧ, wearing disk with uræi . Between his hind legs is a seated female figure, with arms raised and having on her head *śen*, the sun's course; by her side is her name *Ȧuset*, Isis. Behind her are a standard , with human hand and arm, and the signs ?

On the right hand side are "Osiris, great god, prince of the Ȧmenta" (underworld), seated in a shrine, and "Isis, great lady, divine mother, daughter of Rā, mistress of sepulchral meals"; between them is the soul of the deceased offering incense to Osiris. The same scene is repeated on the left hand side, but "Nephthys, the divine sister, daughter of Rā mistress of Ȧmenta," takes the place of Isis, and the deceased, himself offers incense. Round and about the goddess are winged *ut'ats*, *śen*, *ānχ*, etc.

II. The goddess Nut, with outstretched wings, holding *ānχ*, "life," in each hand, winged uræi, uræi, *śen*, and *ut'ats*; over the right wing is inscribed  *Nut urt mest neteru*, "Nut, the great lady, genetrix of the gods," and over the left 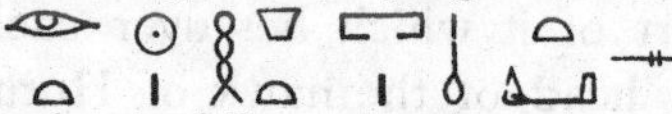 *ȧrit Rā ḥent perχeru ṭāt-s*, "daughter of Rā, mistress of sepulchral meals, may she give . . . . ." On the left hand side of the goddess is a standing figure of the goddess Maāt, pouring out water from a vase for the deceased, "the divine father of Ȧmen, Nesi-pa-ur-shef, triumphant," who kneels below, and receives it in his two hands, out of which he drinks.

Above the goddess are four lines of inscription, which read:—

ȧn Maā se Rā ḥent Ȧmentet

"*Behold Maā, daughter of Rā, Mistress of the underworld.*

seśep - k qebḥ qebḥ ȧb - k ȧm - t

Receive thou cool water, may be refreshed heart thy therewith,

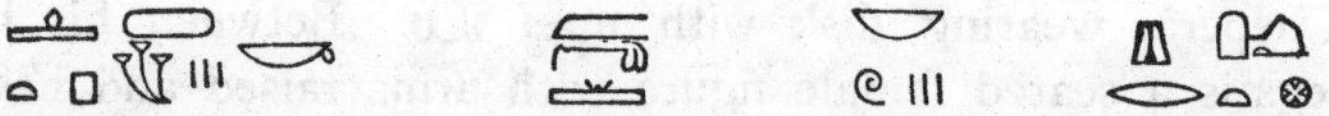

ḥetep - k embaḥ nebu χer-āba

be there offerings to thee in the presence of the lords of Cher-āba,[1]

seqebḥ ȧb-k χer nehi en neb

may be refreshed heart thy under the sycamore tree of the lady of

[1] See Brugsch, *Dict. Géog.*, p. 625. Cher-āba is an old name of Babylon, near On-Heliopolis on the right bank of the Nile.

Ḥeb [1] ṭem ren · k hru neb em pa en

Ḥeb, may be recited name thy day every in the house of

neb mer [2] χennu ba - k tennu hru

the lord of the lake, may alight soul thy every day

χeft Re - stetet per ba · k

opposite Re - stetet,[3] *may come forth soul thy" !*

In front of her is the inscription :—

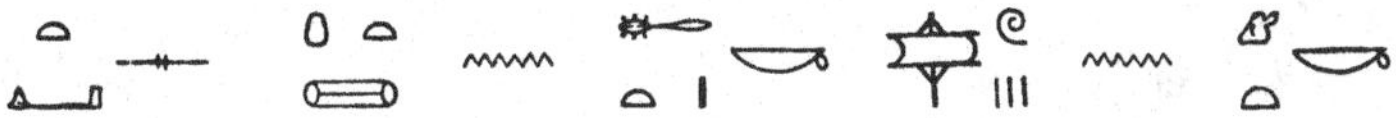

ṭāt - s ta en χat · k nifu en fent-k

May give she food for body thy, air for nose thy,

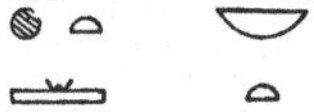

χet nebt

[*and*] *thing every.*

On the right of the goddess Nut is a figure of Maāt pouring out water for the deceased, who kneels at her feet. Above her are four lines of inscription, which read :—

ȧn Maā se Rā ḥent Ȧmentet

" *Behold Maā, daughter of Rā, mistress of the underworld*

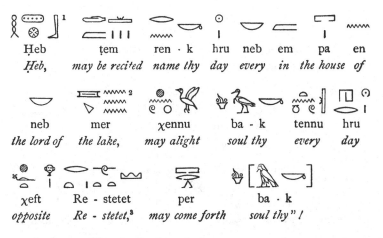

ṭāt - s perχeru sennu ȧḥ apt χa em

May give she sepulchral meals, cakes, oxen, ducks, thousands of

[1] See Brugsch, *Dict. Géog.*, p. 489.

[2] *Ibid.*, p. 273.

[3] *I.e.*, the passage to the tomb.

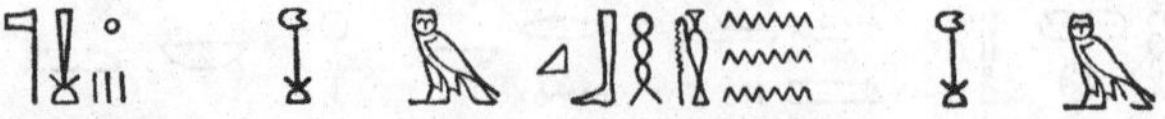

neter sentrȧ χa em qebh χa em
[offerings of] incense, thousands of cool libations, thousands of

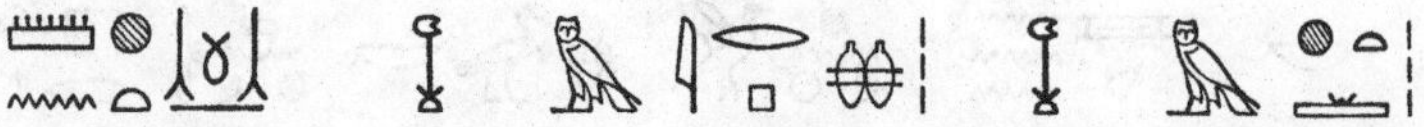

menχet χa em ȧrp χa em χet
linen bandages, thousands of wine, thousands of things

neb nefert ābt χa em χet nebt nefert beneret
all, beautiful, pure ; thousands of things all, beautiful, pleasant

en - ka en
to the ka of . . . . [1] *Nesi-pa-ur-shef.*"

Beneath the goddess Nut are three perpendicular rows of scenes. Those of the centre row are :—

I. Beetle with human arms and hands, wearing disk and uræi , from the necks of which hang ; beneath are *ṭeṭ*, "stability," and *śen*, the sun's course. On each side is Osiris bearded wearing disk.

II. Standard with plumes (*i.e.*, Osiris), on each side of which stands a human-headed hawk wearing ; also winged *ut'at* and uræus with . Beneath are Isis and Nephthys.

III. Beetle with outstretched wings, between his fore-legs disk of the sun, with two serpents, and *śen*, in a boat ; on each side , *śen*, and uræus with .

IV. Standard rising out of *śen*, with two *menȧts* ; on one side winged uræus with disk, *ut'at*, and Nephthys kneeling ; on the other winged uræus with disk, *ut'at*, and Isis. The division between scenes III. and IV. is made by a row of .

[1] Here follows a list of the titles of the deceased.

V. Beetle, with disk of the sun between his fore-legs  ; on each side is the hawk of Horus wearing the crowns of the north and south, and winged *ut'at* with uræus.

VI. Osiris with Isis and Nephthys in the form of winged uræi. Beneath are three mutilated lines of inscription which read :—

1. 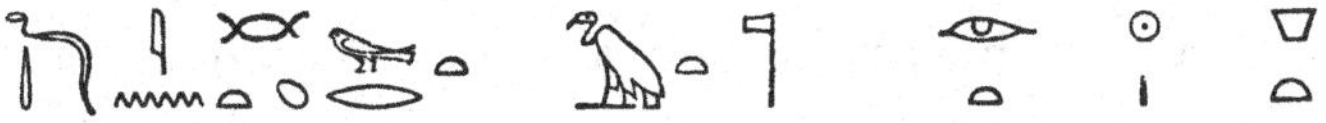

ȧn Net urt mut neter ȧrit Rā ḥent

"*Behold Neith, mighty lady, mother goddess, daughter of Rā, mistress of*

perχeru ṭāt - s unen Ȧusȧr ȧtf neterȧ en

sepulchral meals. May grant she to rise up Osiris, divine father of

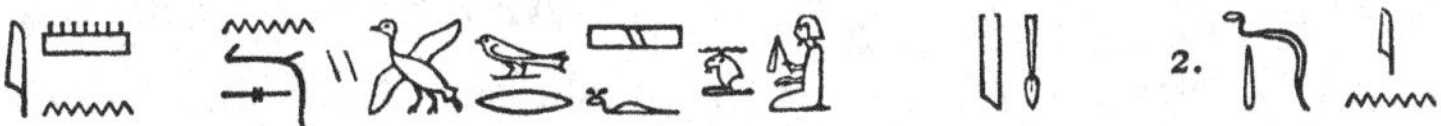

Ȧmen Nesi - pa - ur - shef maātχeru. 2. ȧn

Ȧmen, Nesi - pa - ur - shef, triumphant! Behold

Serqet urt se Rā ānχ ḥer ȧb .....

Serqet, mighty lady, daughter of Rā, living within .....

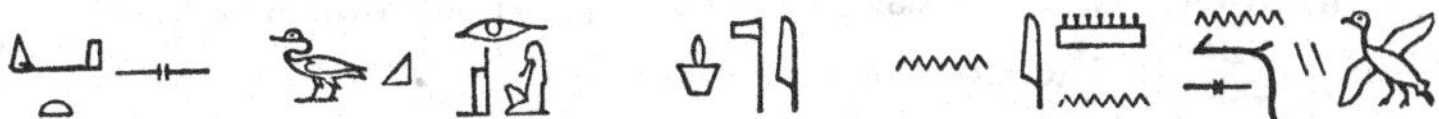

ṭāt - s āq Ȧusȧr ȧtef neterȧ en Ȧmen Nesi - pa -

Gives she to enter Osiris, divine father of Ȧmen, Nesi - pa -

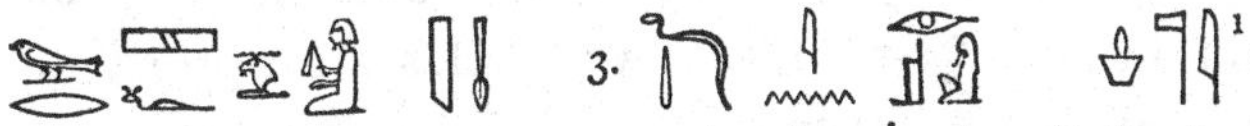 [1] etc......

ur - shef maātχeru 3. ȧn Ȧusȧr ȧtef neterȧ

ur - shef, triumphant! Behold Osiris, divine father," etc.

[1] Here follows a complete list of the titles of the deceased as given on page 9. The speech, etc., which is put into his mouth runs round the edge of the foot of the coffin ; it is much mutilated, and only enough of it remains to show that he prayed for sepulchral offerings.

The set of scenes on the right hand side of the cover is as follows:—

I. Osiris and Isis in a shrine. Inscriptions *Ȧusȧr neb ḥeḥ Un-nefer neter āa ḥeq ānχ*, "Osiris, lord of eternity, Un-nefer, god great, prince of life." *Ȧuset urt ḥent Ȧmentet ṭāt-s ḥetep*, "Isis, great lady, mistress of the underworld. May she give an offering." Before the shrine stands *Maāt ḥent Ȧmentet*, "Maāt the mistress of Ȧmenta," giving the deceased his heart, .

II. The god Ptaḥ-Seker-Ȧusȧr, wearing *atef* crown, and "Nephthys, divine sister, daughter of Rā, mistress of sepulchral meals, may she give an offering," *Nebt-ḥet neter sent ȧrit Rā ḥent perχeru ṭā-s ḥetep*, in a shrine. In front of the shrine is the goddess Maāt[1] giving a vase of cool water to the deceased.

III. Ram wearing disk and plumes , and Isis in a shrine. In front of the shrine deceased adoring Maāt.

IV. Standard, with disk and plumes, emblem of Osiris, and Nephthys in a shrine. In front of the shrine stands the lion-headed "goddess of Ȧmenta," whose name is effaced, giving to the deceased.

The set of scenes on the left hand side is as follows:—

I. Isis and Nephthys in a shrine. In front of the shrine stands the deceased by the side of an altar making an offering of incense to Maāt, who holds a sceptre in her right hand, and in her left.

II. The god *Ptaḥ Seker Ausȧr neter āa*, "Ptaḥ-Seker Ȧusȧr, great god," in the form of a hawk,

[1] *Maāt ḥent Ȧmentet ṭāt ḥetep*, "Maāt, mistress of the underworld, may she give an offering."

wearing the *atef* crown with plumes, disk, and uræi, , and Isis in a shrine. In front of the shrine is the deceased adoring Maāt and presenting offerings.

III. Horned ram wearing disk, plumes, and uræi,  *neter āa ānχ maāt*, "the great god, living by law," and Nephthys in a shrine. In front of the shrine is the deceased offering fruit, flowers, cakes, and jars of wine to Maāt.

IV. Standard, with disk and plumes, emblem of "Osiris, lord of eternity," Isis, and three (*sic*) children of Horus, standing on a lotus flower, in a shrine. In front of the shrine is the goddess Maāt, pouring out water  upon a hand of the deceased. On the projecting foot of the coffin cover are two scenes in which Isis and Nephthys are represented kneeling by the side of a table of offerings before the god Osiris, "lord of Abydos, prince of Åmenta" (underworld), who wears the *atef* crown. The five lines of inscription above Isis read:—["Behold Isis the divine sister,"]

t'eṭ	set	ren - nek	senti	ur	åu
says	*she,*	*Weep for thee*	*the two sisters*	*mighty ones!*	*Is*

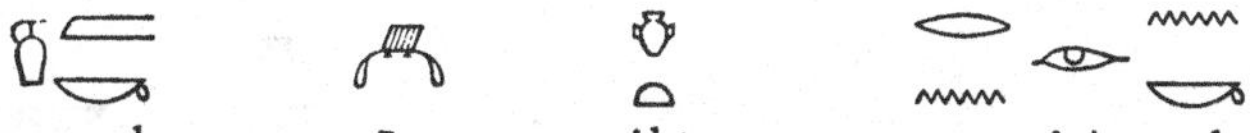

χnem-k	āu	åbt	ren åri - nek
united with thee	*joy of*	*heart!*	*A weeping make for thee*

mesu	en	pa - k	t'amu	en	nut - k
the children	*of*	*house thy,*	*the young people*	*of*	*town thy*

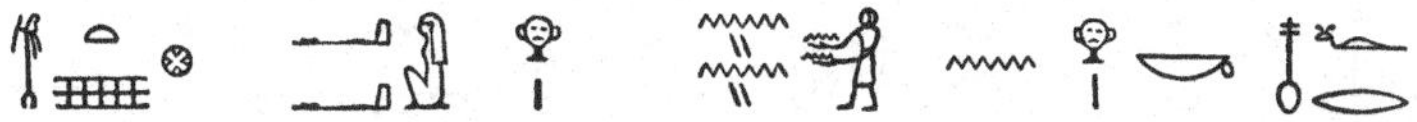

Uast	āāui - å	ḥer	nini	en	ḥrå - k	nefer
Thebes.	*Two hands my [are]*		*paying homage*	*to*	*face thy*	*beautiful.*

mer-k bener en χat - á ter em ḥeq

Love thy is pleasant to body my, O hailed as prince

āu áb Merti ḥer ...... áu

of joy of the heart, Merti, president of ...... Is

śef-k em taiu nebu em ḥeq taiu

terror (awe) thy in lands all as prince of the world!

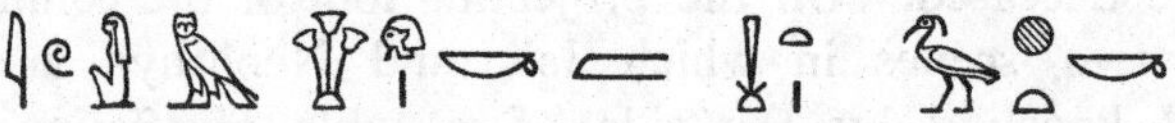

áu - á em ḥa - k em sent χut - k

I am behind thee as a sister protecting thee."

The seven mutilated lines above Nephthys read:—

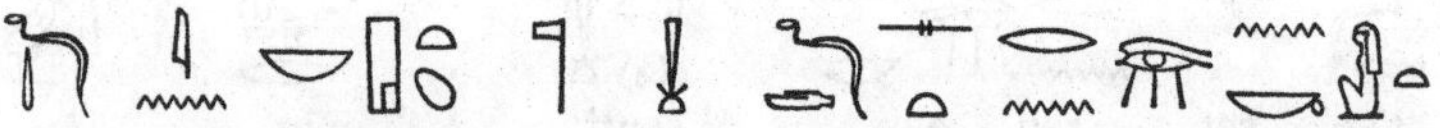

án Nebt-ḥet neter sent t'eṭ-set ren - nek - á

"*Behold Nephthys, divine sister, says she, Weep for thee I,*

en neb áb - á χer ment nuk set-k

for the lord of heart my, with anguish. I am daughter thy,

mer - k rer - á pa - k āāui - á ḥer ṭep - á

beloved thy, go round I house thy, two hands my [are] on head my

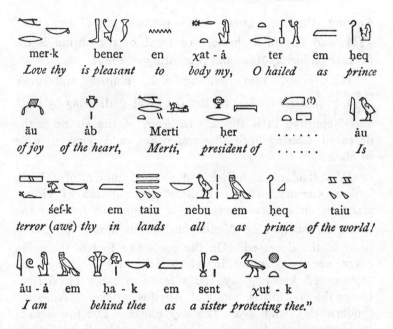

má árit-á en Un-nefer t'eṭ - á - nek enti em

as did I for Un-nefer. Say I to thee what is in

àb - à	. . . .	renem - nek	pet	ḥer	amt	
heart my.		*Weeps for thee*	*heaven,*	*streaming with*	*tears*	

set	àkeb - nek	χabesu	àm set	t'etta
is it,	*lament for thee*	*the stars*	*in it*	*for ever"!*

The remaining space is filled with two scenes in which the soul of the deceased is represented adoring Anubis.

Above the two outside sets of scenes are ten lines of inscription which read :—

Left side: 1. 2. 3. 4. 5.

Right side: 1. 2. 3. 4. 5.

Left side. 1. *Met àmχi χer Àusàr neb Àmentet.* 2. *Met àmχi χer Ptaḥ-Sekeri.* 3. *Met àmχi χer ba āa ānχ Nut.* . . . . 4. *Met àmχi χer Ṭuamāutef maātχeru.* 5. *Met àmχi χer Àuset ur mut neter ṭāt-s ḥetep t'efau χet nebt.* Right side. 1. *Met àmχi χer Àusàr neb Àbṭu.* 2. *Met àmχi χer Ptaḥ-Sekeri.* 3. *Àmχi χer ba āa ānχ em.* . . . . . 4. *Met àmχi χer Àusàr neb Ta-sert.* 5. *Met àmχi χer Mesthà neter āa neb Àmentet χenti Re-stetet maātχeru.*

No regular order appears to have been followed by the artist in painting the outside of this cover. We should expect pictures of the four children of Horus, and of Anubis and Apuat; neither of these two last gods is mentioned, nor Ḥāpi.

Around the edge of the cover are two horizontal lines of inscription which read :—

I. 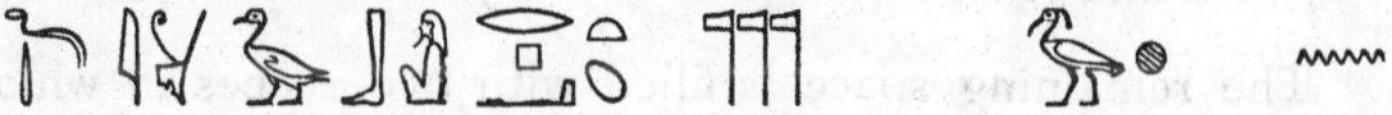

ȧn Seb erpāt neteru χu en

"*Behold Seb, the erpā of the gods, glorifying*

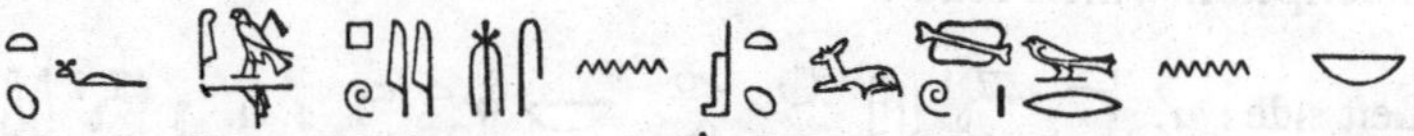

se - f Ḥeru, pui mes en Ȧuset āuur en neb

son his Horus this born of Isis, heir of the lord of

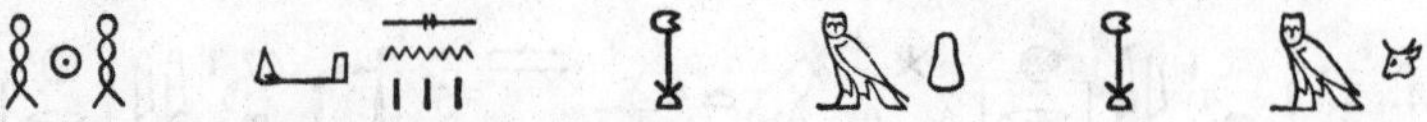

ḥeḥ ṭā - sen χa em ta χa em ȧḥ

eternity. May grant they thousands of cakes, thousands of oxen,

χa em apṭ χa neter sentrȧ em χa met em

thousands of ducks, thousands of incense, thousands of oil,

χa em merḥet χa em ȧrp χa em

thousands of wax, thousands of wine, thousands of

ȧrt χa em menχet χa em renpet

milk, thousands of linen bandages, thousands of flowers of

neb χa em χet neb nefer āb χet neb

all kinds, thousands of things all beautiful, pure; things all

nefer bener enti ānχ neteru ȧm - sen ȧn Ȧusȧr
beautiful, pleasant which live the gods on them, to Osiris,

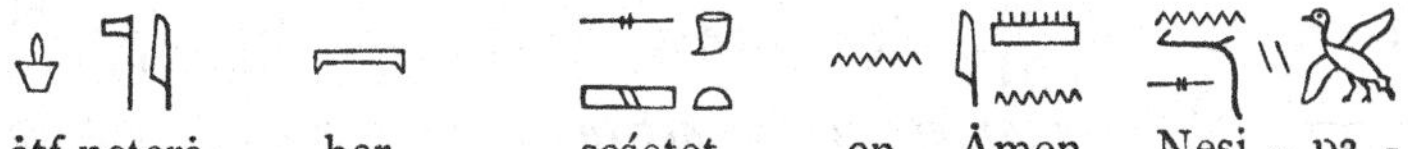

ȧtf neterȧ ḥer seśetet en Ȧmen Nesi - pa -
divine father, president of the mysteries of Ȧmen, Nesi - pa -

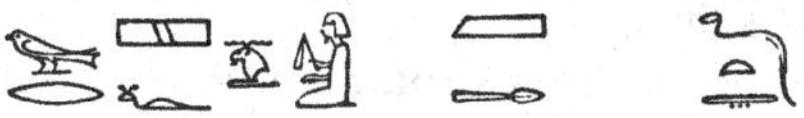

ur - śef maātχeru t'etta
ur - śef, triumphant for ever!

II. 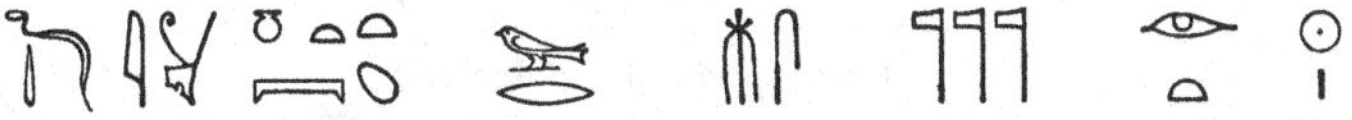

Met ȧn Nut ur mes neteru ȧrit Rā
Behold Nut, mighty lady, genetrix of the gods, daughter of Rā,

ḥeq taiu Ḥeru pui mes en Ȧuset āuuā
prince of the world, and Horus this born of Isis, heir

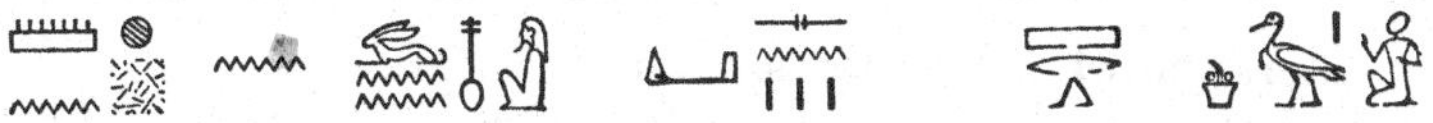

menχ en Unnefer ṭā - sen per ba - ȧ
perfect of Unnefer, may grant they to come out soul my,

. . . . u ba - ȧ . . . . mȧ neteru śesi
. . . . *soul my* . . . . *like the gods following*

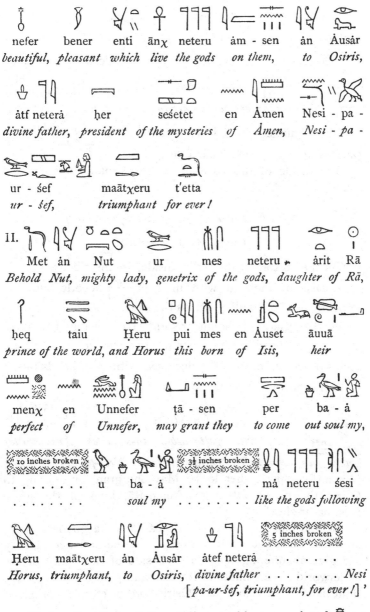

Ḥeru maātχeru ȧn Ȧusȧr ȧtef neterȧ . . . .
Horus, triumphant, to Osiris, divine father . . . . *Nesi*
[*pa-ur-śef, triumphant, for ever!*] '

Under the foot of the coffin outside are painted *ṭeṭ*, emblem of stability, winged uræi, *ut'ats*, Nephthys with uplifted arms and hands, seated on , winged *ut'ats* and uræi, double standard , and the four children of Horus, viz., *Mesθȧ*, "great god, lord of the underworld," human-headed; *Ḥāpi*, ape-headed; *Ṭuamāutef neter āa neb ṭuat*, "Ṭuamāutef, great god, lord of the underworld," jackal-headed; and *Qebḥsennuf*, Qebḥsennuf, hawk-headed.

The inside of this cover is neither ornamented nor inscribed.

IV. *The Inner Coffin of Nesi-pa-ur-shef.*

(Description of the Inside.)

On the bottom of the coffin, inside, are inscribed:—

I. Disk of the sun with uræi, , beetle, and two serpents in a boat sailing across the sky.

II. The "lady of the underworld" (*ṭuat*), winged, wearing upon her head. Above her are two winged uræi, and on each side of her head is the deceased with both hands raised in adoration of the goddess. The inscription reads:—

 *Set χeft neb-s ṭā-s ḥetep Ȧusȧr ȧtef neterȧ en Ȧmen-Rā, suten neteru Nesi-pa-ur-śef*, "Set (Amenta) opposite her lord. May she grant an offering to Osiris, the divine father of Ȧmen-Rā, king of the gods, Nesi-pa-ur-shef."

Behind each figure of the deceased is the goddess Maāt, and the inscription, "Maāt, mistress of the underworld, may she give an offering"![1] On each side of the "lady of the underworld" is a standard with disk and plumes: that on the right hand is described as "Osiris, lord of eternity, prince of

[1] 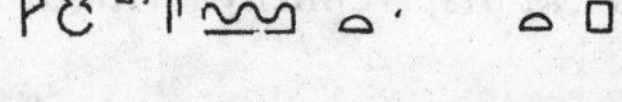 *Maāt ḥenut Ȧmentet ṭāt-s ḥetep.*

everlasting,"[1] and that on the left, "Osiris, lord of eternity, prince of everlasting, traversing millions of years during the period of his life."[2] Before the standard on the right hand is a the table of offerings, by the side of which stands "Nephthys, divine sister, daughter of Rā, mistress of the beautiful house (*i.e.*, the tomb), giving an offering of all fair and pure things";[3] and before the standard on the left hand is also a table of offerings, by the side of which stands "Isis, the great lady, divine mother, mistress of the beautiful house, giving an offering."[4] Beneath this, on each side, is the soul of Osiris (the deceased) in the form of a human-headed, bearded bird, with a hand raised in adoration of the goddess; by its side is a winged *ut'at* with an uræus. The emblem of the east, *Àbṭu*, is on the right hand, and that of the west, *Àmenta*, on the left hand. Beneath the right wing of the goddess of the underworld are:—1, Bearded, green-faced, human-headed god called  *Àtmu neb Ànnu neter āa ḥet āa*, "Àtmu, lord of Heliopolis, great god of the great house"; 2, bearded, red-faced, human-headed god called  *Shu*, Shu; 3, god with on his head, called  *se Rā*, "the child of Rā"; 4, uræus, with on his head; and 5, soul of the deceased by the side of a table of offerings making an offering of incense. Beneath the left wing of the goddess are:—1, hawk-headed god 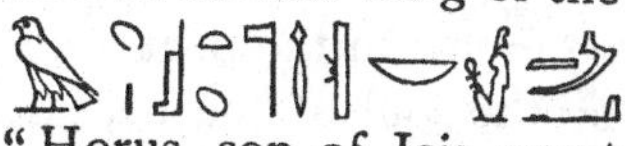 *Ḥeru se Àuset neter āa neb Maāt*, "Horus, son of Isis, great

1 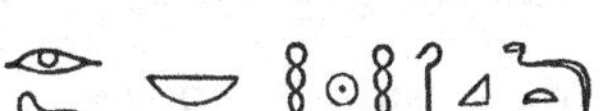 *Àusàr neb ḥeḥ ḥeq t'etta.*

2 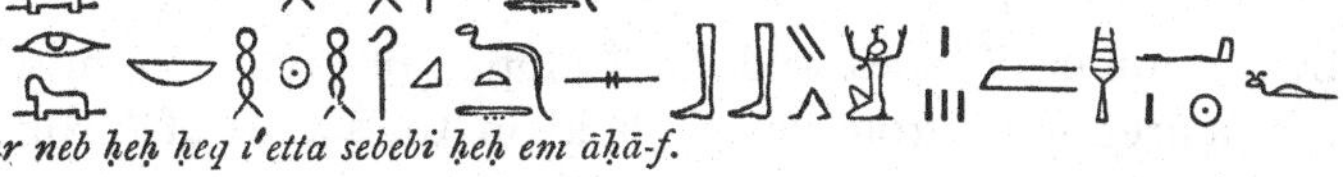 *Àusàr neb ḥeḥ ḥeq t'etta sebebi ḥeḥ em āḥā-f.*

3  *met àn Nebt ḥet neter sent àrit Rā ḥenut pa nefer ṭāt-s ḥetep χet neb nefer āb.*

4 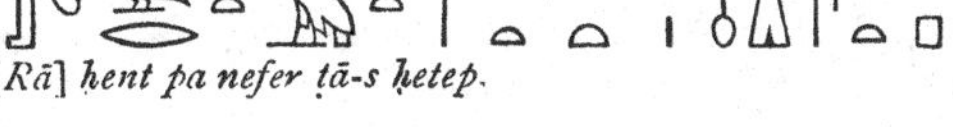 *Àuset urt mut neter àrit [Rā] ḥent pa nefer ṭā-s ḥetep.*

god, lord of law"; 2, god with on his head; 3, uræus , with on his head; and 4, soul of the deceased offering incense .

III. Boat of the sun, accompanied by the *àbṭu* and *ànṭu* fishes, on the prow a bird . In the boat are the goddess Maāt, a goddess wearing disk and horns , Shu the great god,[1] the cynocephalus ape of Thoth, wearing , emblematic of disk and crescent moon; Rā, seated, holding flail and in his hands; "Isis, divine sister, mistress of the underworld,"[2] and a god who rows the boat along with hawk-headed oars. Above the boat, on the right hand and on the left, is a winged uræus, and . The boat is supported by the hands of two ram-headed gods. The inscription relating to him on the right hand reads:—

neter pen ḥer àat neter āa

God this (is) chief of the sarcophagus, god great;

and that to the god on the left hand:—

neter pen ur em ṭuat neter āa neb Àmentet

God this (is) great in the underworld, god great, lord of the underworld.

Beneath the boat are a beetle-headed god and disk adored by the soul of the deceased,[3] and the hawk of Horus; above are winged *ut'ats.* The beetle-headed god stands upon a circle in which the double disk of the sun is being adored by a number of apes, and is enveloped in rays of light which are poured forth from vessels held in the hands of "Nut, the

1  *Śu neter āa.*

2 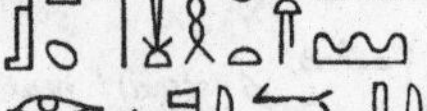 *Àuset neter sent ḥenut Àmentet.*

3 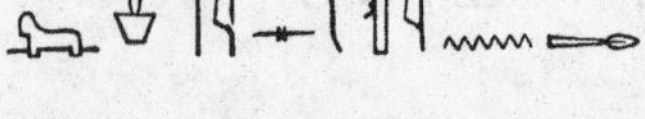 *Àusàr neter àtf Nesi-Àmen maātχeru.*

great lady, genetrix of the gods,"[1] and "[Isis], mighty goddess in the underworld, mistress of Åmenta."[2] Below is repeated *ut'at neb neferu,* "ut'at, lord of beauties," and a lion-headed goddess stands on each side of the circle.

IV. "Shu, great god, lord of the underworld."[3] On the right hand are Nephthys and a ram-headed god holding, and on the left are Isis and a ram-headed god holding.

On the sides, at the head of the coffin, are painted :—

The soul of the deceased in the form of a human-headed hawk, accompanied by Isis and Nephthys in the form of winged uræi wearing disks, and the four canopic jars which contain the intestines from the body of the deceased. Under each wing is Anubis, jackal-headed, wearing the crowns of the north and the south, with, and before him is the sceptre, with double *menåt*, offerings, and winged *ut'at.* The inscription above him reads, "May Anubis, great god, mighty one in the underworld, chief in Neter-χert (the underworld), and in the coffin, president of Åmenta, give all things good and pure, all things good and pleasant and an offering of *t'efa* food."[4] On the right hand is Anubis seated, and on the left is the god Cheperå,[5] the great god, the "self-produced," beetle-headed.

1  *Nut urt mest neteru.*

2 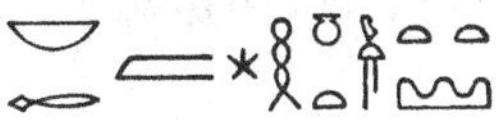 *Neb āa em ṭuat ḥenut Åmentet.*

3  *Šu neter āa neb ṭuat.*

4 
Ånpu neter āa ur em ṭuat ḥer em Neter-χert åm ut χenti en Åmentet ṭā-f χet neb nefer āb χet neb nefer bener ḥetep t'efau.

5  *Cheperå neter āa.*

On the right hand side of the coffin are painted :—

I. The god Ptaḥ-Seker-Àusàr, hawk-headed, holding ; above him is inscribed, "Ptaḥ-Seker-Ausàr within the hidden chamber";[1] "Thoth, lord of divine words, great god, lord of the underworld,"[2] ibis-headed, wearing crown , and standing by the side of a table of offerings; and "Nephthys, divine sister, daughter of Rā, mistress of the underworld," holding in her right hand. These three divine beings are asked to "grant offerings of flowers and fruit and *t'efa* food, and all pleasant things" to the deceased.[3]

II. 1, Horned lion-headed god *Qaba*; 2, human-headed god (?) *Net'et*; 3, human-headed god *Àmu-āa*; 4, bee-headed god *Bennet χeper t'esef*; "Bennet, the self-produced"; 5, ape-headed god *Àmen-en-ṭuat*; 6, ape-headed god *Naḥi*; 7, goddess *Àuset neter sent*, "Isis the divine sister"; and 8, *Nebt-ḥet*, "Nephthys."

III. Disk of the sun on the horizon, and in it deceased standing on steps adoring a ram-headed god, above which is written *Senek*. Behind is Isis or Nephthys, in the form of a winged serpent, wearing disk.

IV. The three gods Bennu, the self-produced, Ḥāpi and Qebḥsennuf, and inscriptions entreating them to give offerings

[1] *Met àn Ptaḥ-Seker-Àusàr ḥer àb Šetaθet.*

[2] *Teḥuti neb neter t'eṭṭu neter āa neb Àmentet.*

[3] *ṭāt-sen ḥetep sennu t'efau χet neb bener.*

of food to the deceased.[1] Each god holds the crook and flail, and has an altar with lotus flowers and before him.

V. "Horus, the avenger of his father,"[2] wearing crowns of the north and south, holding in his hands; "Nut, great lady, genetrix of the gods,"[3] in the form of a woman-headed buckle; Osiris ram-headed; and "Isis, divine sister, mistress of the [beautiful] house."[4]

VI. Standard, with disk and plumes, emblem of Osiris and kneeling figure of Nephthys before a table of offerings.

Above are six lines of inscription which read:—

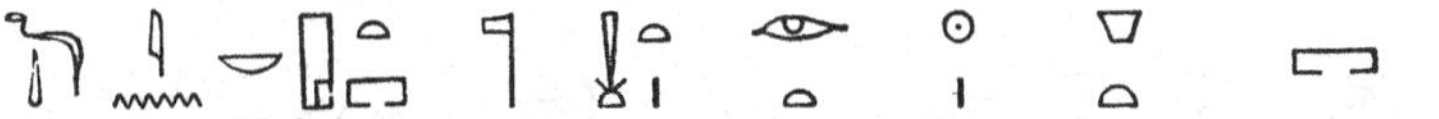

ȧn Neb-ḥet neter sent ȧrit Rā ḥent pa

"Behold Nephthys, divine sister, daughter of Rā, mistress of the house

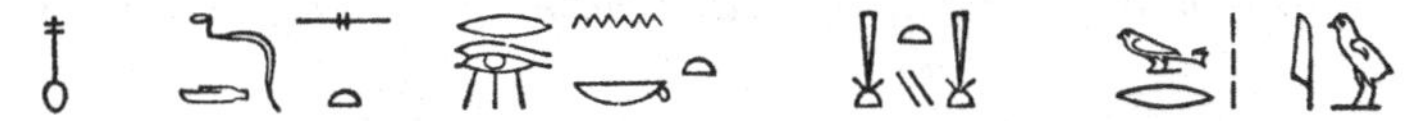

nefer t'eṭ - set, ren - nek senti ur ȧu

beautiful, says she,— Weep for thee the two sisters mighty, is

χnem k āu ȧb ren - nek mesu en

united with thee joy of heart. Weep for thee the children of

1  *Bennu χeper t'esef*

ṭā-f χet neb nefer āb Ḥāpi neter āa neb Ȧmentet ṭā-f ḥetep t'efau Qebḥsenu ṭā-f ta ȧrp.

2 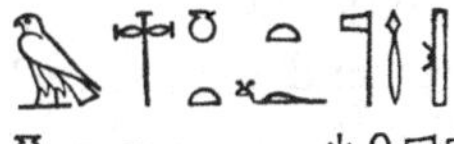

3 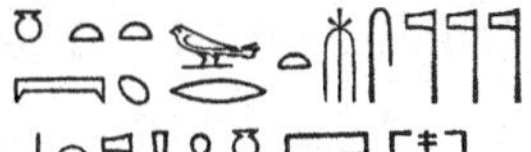

4 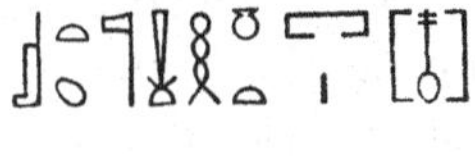

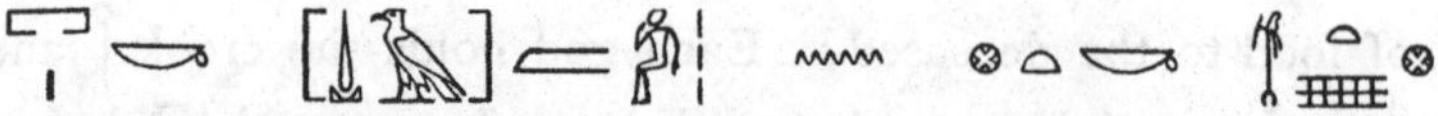

pa - k t'am en nut - k Uast

house thy and the young men of town thy Thebes.

āāui - ȧ ḥer nini en ḥrȧ - k nefer

Two hands my are paying homage to face thy beautiful.

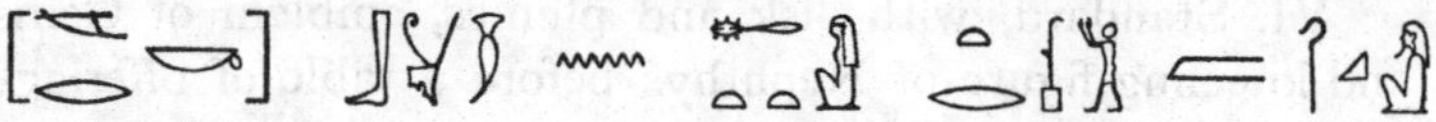

mer - k bener en χat - ȧ ter em ḥeq

Love thy (is) pleasant to body my, O hailed as prince

āu ȧb merti ḥer . . . . . . ȧu śef-k

of joy of heart, Merti, president of the . . . . . Is awe thy

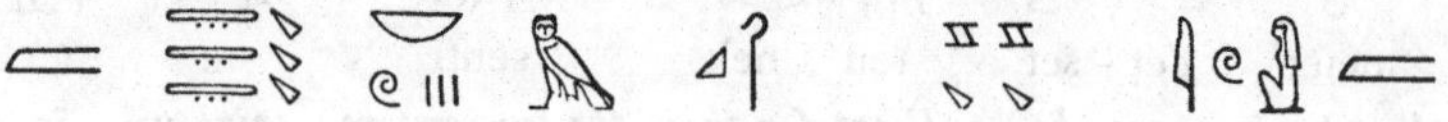

em taiu nebu em ḥeq taiu ȧu - ȧ em

in lands all, as prince of the world. I am

ḥa - k em sent se - k Ḥeru em ne'tet

behind thee as a sister, and son thy Horus as an avenger

ḥrȧ-k er ṭer χeft - k nebu

of thee, to destroy enemies thy all."

On the left hand side of the coffin are painted :—

I. Osiris, wearing crown with plumes and disk, to whom is offered  by Anubis, a table of offerings, and Isis. The inscriptions read, "May Osiris, lord of eternity, prince of everlasting, traversing millions of years during the period of his life, grant an offering of *t'efa* food ; may Isis, mighty lady,

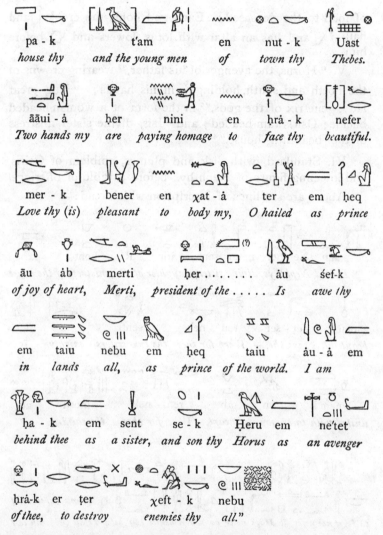

divine mother, daughter of Rā, mistress of the beautiful house, grant all good and pure things, and oil and bandages for Osiris in the coffin, the great god; may Anubis, the great god, mighty one in the underworld, chief in Neter-χert and in the coffin, at the head of Ȧmenta, grant linen bandages for Osiris Nesi-pa-ur-shef[1] triumphant"!

II. 1, Man-headed god *Ȧmen-ḥā*, surrounded by rays of light; 2, horned goat-headed god *Serqet*, 3, bearded god wearing disk; 4, god *Rekḥ*, with head of flame; 5, the god *Cheperȧ* beetle-headed; 6, hawk-headed god *Uben;* 7, horned, man-headed god *Keti;* and 8, cat-headed god *Mȧ*.

III. Disk of the sun on the horizon, and in it deceased adoring a horned hawk wearing a disk, above which is written *Ba en Rā*, "the soul of Rā." Behind are a winged serpent, *ut'ats*, and .

IV. The three gods Nefer-Ȧtmu, Mesθȧ and Ṭuamāutef, and inscriptions entreating them to give offerings of food to

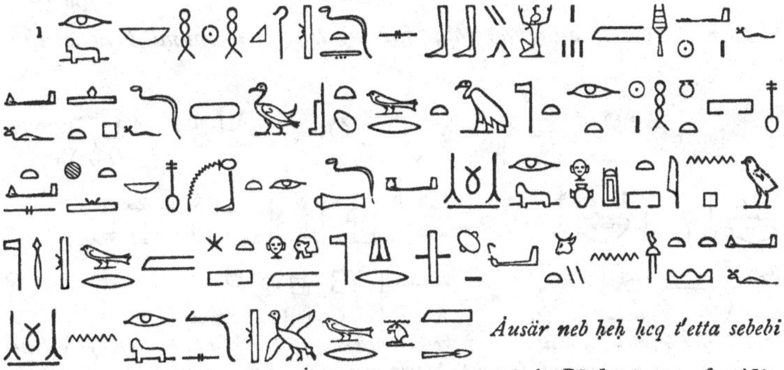

Ȧusȧr neb ḥeḥ ḥcq t'etta sebebi ḥeḥ em āḥā-f ṭā-f ḥetep t'efa Ȧuset urt mut netert ȧrit Rā ḥent pa nefer ṭāt-s χet neb nefer ābt mat' menχet Ȧusȧr ḥer ȧb ȧat Ȧnpu neter āa ur em ṭuat ḥetep em neter χert ȧm ut χenti en Amentet ṭā-f menχet en Ȧusȧr Nesi-pa-ur-šef maātχeru.

the deceased.[1] Each god holds the crook and whip, and has an altar with lotus flowers and before him.

V. A ṭeṭ, crowned with on each side of which is a table of offerings, Isis and Nephthys holding in each hand, and "Thoth, lord of divine words, scribe of the gods,"[2] ibis-headed, wearing the *atef* crown.

VI. Standard, with disk and plumes, emblem of Osiris, and kneeling figure of Isis before a table of offerings. Above are five lines of inscription which read:—

ȧn Ȧuset urt mut neter ȧrit Rā ḥent

"*Behold Isis, mighty lady, divine mother, daughter of Rā, mistress*

Ȧmentet t'eṭ - set renem - ȧ nek ȧb - ȧ χer

of the underworld, says she, Weep I for thee, heart my hath

ment nuk set - k mert - k rer - ȧ pa - k

pain. I am daughter thy, darling thy. Go round I house thy,

1 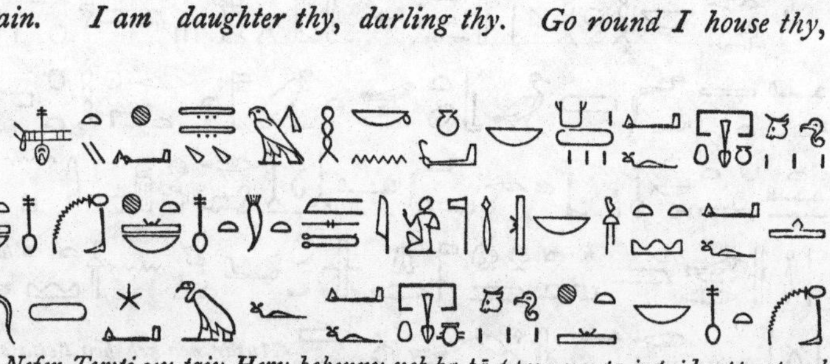

Nefer Temti χu taiu Ḥeru ḥekennu neb ka ṭā-f perχeru ta ȧrt ȧḥ apt χet neb nefer āb χet neb nefert beneret Mesθȧ neter āa neb Amentet ṭā-f ḥetep t'ef Tuamāutef ṭā-f, etc.

2 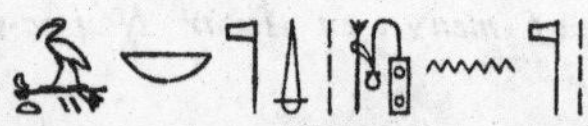

āāui - à ḥer ṭep - à mà àrit - nà en Un-nefer
two hands my [are] on head my as did I for Unnefer.

t'eṭ - à nek enti em àb - à nuk senti ur
Say I to thee what [is] in heart my, I, the sister mighty.

renem - nek pet ḥer set àkeb - nek
Weeps for thee heaven, streaming with tears [is] it; lament for thee

χabesu àm set t'eṭ - sen k pa neb en Qamt
the stars in it, and say they to thee, O lord of Egypt,

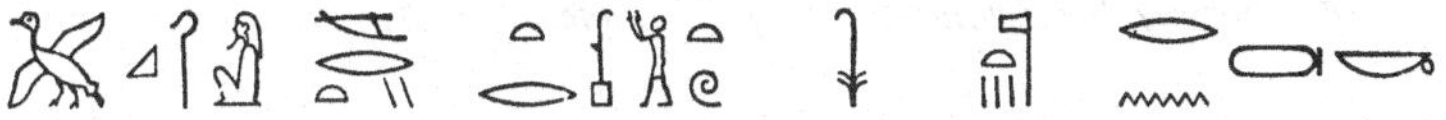

pa ḥeq merti ter - tu suten neteru ren - k
O prince beloved, adored art thou as king of gods, name thy

seqa ur Ḥeru pui χāā em ḥe't
exalts greatly Horus this, diademed with the white crown.

se - k χer em maātχeru
Son thy speaketh with triumph"!

At the foot are painted a *teṭ*, emblem of Osiris, wearing plumes, disk and horns, Isis and Nephthys each in the form of a buckle, a man-headed, and a rat (?)-headed god. The inscriptions entreat these gods to give gifts of *t'efa* food to the deceased.

V. *The Inner Coffin of Nesi-pa-ur-shef.*

(Description of the Outside.)

The outside of the coffin is inscribed and ornamented as follows. The top edge is ornamented with a row of uræi, beneath which are two lines of inscription which, beginning over the head and continuing along each side, read :—

I. 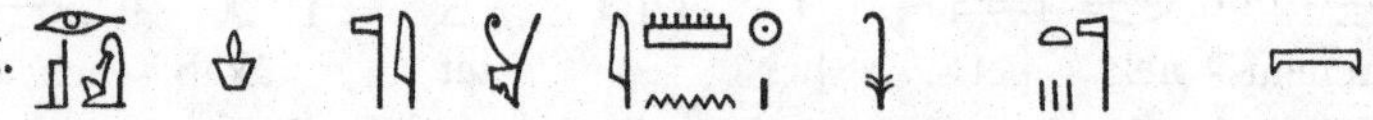

Ȧusȧr ȧtef neterȧ en Ȧmen-Rā suten neteru ḥer

"Osiris, father divine of Ȧmen-Rā, king of the gods, president

ān neter ḥet en Ȧmen - pa Nesi - pa - ur -

of the scribes of the divine house of the Ȧmen temple, Nesi - pa - ur -

śef maātχeru t'eṭ - f ȧnet' ḥrȧ-k Ȧusȧr χenti

shef, triumphant! Says he, Hail to thee, Osiris, at the head

Ȧmentet Un-nefer ḥeq ānχiu suten ḥeḥ neb

of Ȧmentet, Unnefer, prince of the living, king of eternity, lord of

t'etta sebebi ḥeḥ em āḥā - f

everlasting, traversing millions of years during life his,

χāā - f Ȧuset ḥer unam - f Neb - ḥet ḥer

diademed is he with Isis on right hand his and Nephthys on

åbṭ - f se Rā em sa ṭep - f ḥer

left hand his, and the son of Rā as a protector of head his, to

nini en ḥrå-f nefer Ånpu χenti saḥ

adore face his beautiful; [hail] Anubis, at the head of the hall

neter ḥet neteru nebu Ta-sert ṭā - sen

of the divine house; [hail] gods all of Tasert; may grant they

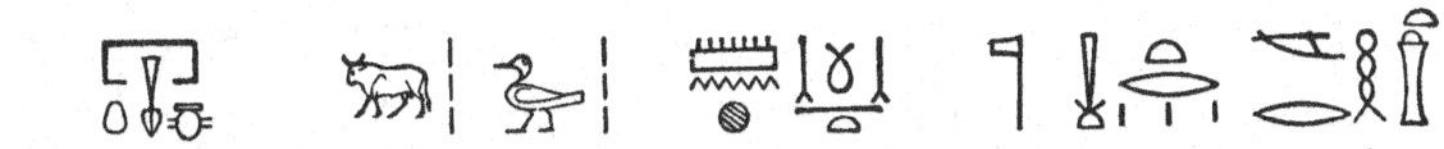

perχeru åḥ apt menχet neter sentrå merḥ

sepulchral meals, oxen, ducks, linen bandages, incense, wax,

qebḥ årp årt χet neb nefert ābtet χet

libations, wine, milk, things all beautiful, pure, things

neb nefer bener em ṭāt en pet qema

all beautiful, pleasant, of the giving of heaven, of the production

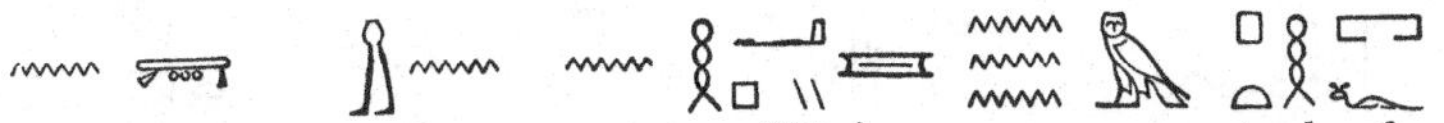

en ta ån en Ḥāpi em teph - f

of earth, of the bringing of Nile from cavern his,

en Ausår uā åten en t'ebā maāt en Uast āb

to Osiris, only one, vicar of the seal (?) of law of Thebes, priest,

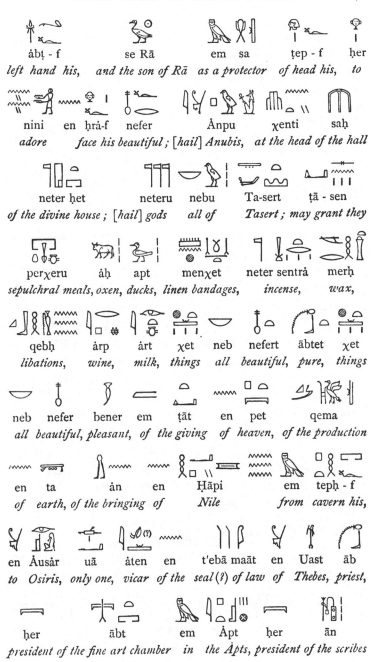

ḥer ābt em Åpt ḥer ān

president of the fine art chamber in the Åpts, president of the scribes

neter ḥet en Ȧmen-Rā suten neteru Nesi - pa - ur -
of the divine house of Ȧmen-Rā, king of the gods, Nesi - pa - ur -

śef maātχeru
shef, triumphant"!

II. 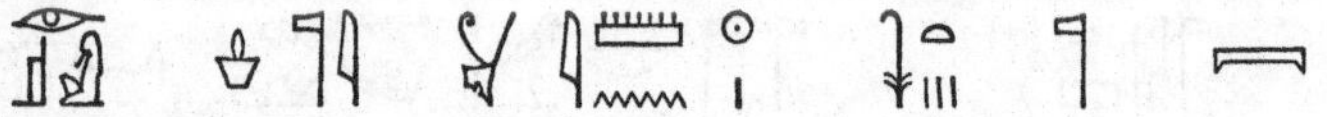

Ȧusȧr ȧtef neterȧ en Ȧmen-Rā, suten neteru ḥer
"*Osiris, father divine of Ȧmen-Rā, king of the gods, president*

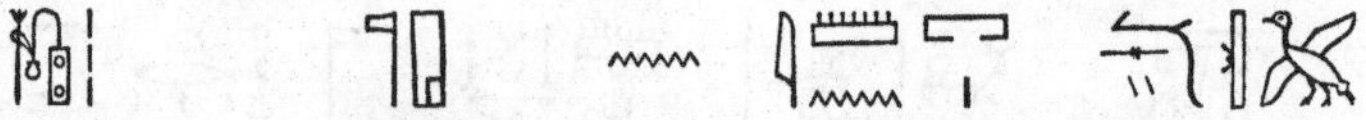

ān neter ḥet en Ȧmen - pa Nesi - pa -
of the scribes of the divine house of the Ȧmen temple, Nesi - pa -

ur - śef maātχeru t'eṭ - f ȧnet' ḥrȧ-ten naiu
ur - shef, triumphant! Says he, Hail to you, O ye

nebu Ȧmentet paut neteru āat ȧmi
lords of the underworld, and [you] cycle of gods great in

Neter-χert ḥetepi enti em ṭuat
the underworld, and ye resting ones who are in the underworld,

st'eri neteri baiu ānχiu enti en
ye who are reposing, ye mighty souls, ye living ones who are in

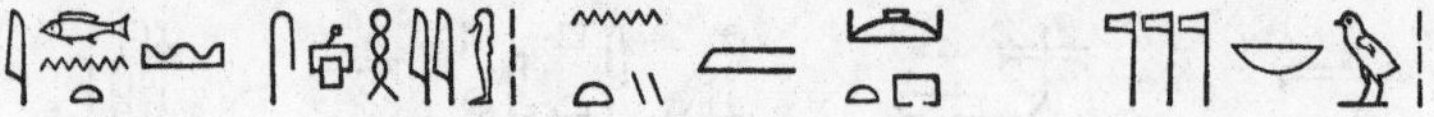

Ȧnt saḥi enti em ȧat neteru nebu
the grave, ye mummies who are in the tomb, [hail] gods all of

Ta-sert māi - ten åri - ten en Åusår åtef neterå en

Tasert, come ye, protect ye Osiris, father divine of

Åmen-Rā suten neteru Nesi - pa - ur - śef maātχeru

Åmen-Rā, king of the gods, Nesi - pa - ur - shef, triumphant!

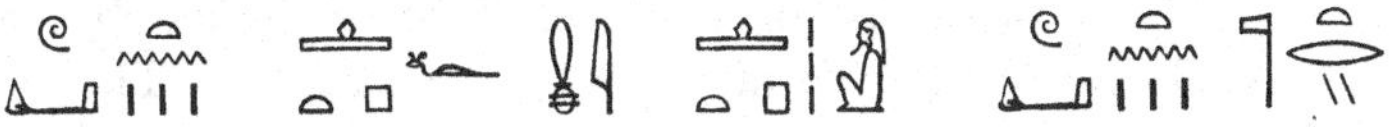

ṭāu-ten ḥetep - f må ḥetep ṭāu-ten neteri

Grant ye that may rest he as those who rest. Grant ye might

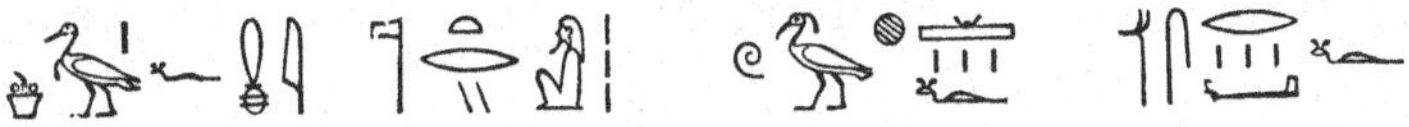

ba - f må neteriu χu - f user - f

to soul his like the mighty ones. May be mighty he, may be powerful he

χer paut neteru āat nebu ḥet per

before the cycle of the gods great, lords of the temple. May come forth

āq - f ån śenā - f ḥer sbau sebeχet

and enter he, may be without repulse he at the doors and the pylons

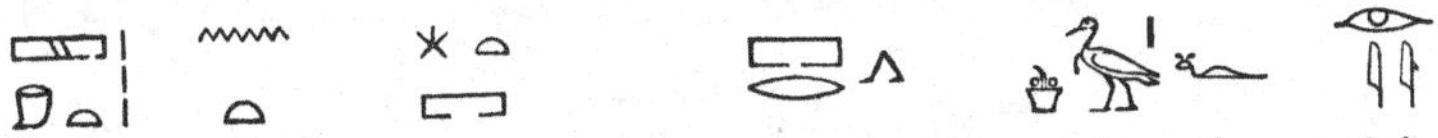

śeta ent ṭuat per ba - f åri

secret of the underworld. May come forth soul his to do

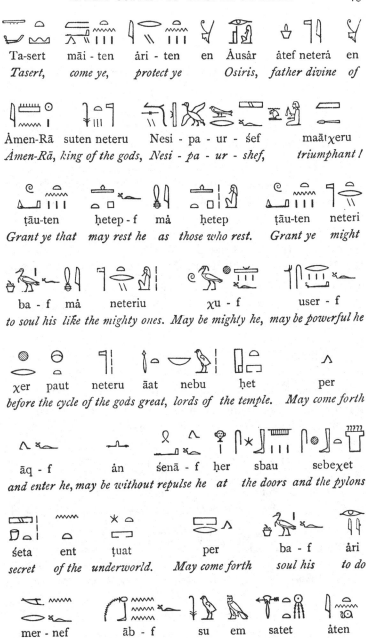

mer - nef āb - f su em satet åten

what wishes he. May refresh he himself in the beams of the disk,

en Ȧusȧr āb ḥer ābt neter ḥet en

Osiris, priest, president of the fine art chamber, divine house of the

Ȧmen-pa ȧtef neterȧ āb en Ȧmen Nesi - pa - ur - śef

Ȧmen temple, father divine, priest of Ȧmen, Nesi - pa - ur - shef."

On the rounded end of the coffin is painted a figure of Nut, " the genetrix of the gods," accompanied by Isis and Nephthys in the form of winged serpents. The line of inscription on the right hand entreats Nephthys to grant to the deceased sepulchral offerings of the best, and in that on the left Isis is entreated to do the same. Beneath Nut are the four children of Horus, Mesθȧ, Ḥāpi, Ṭuamāutef, and Qebḥsennuf, and two figures of  *Nefer Atmu χui taui*, " Nefer Atmu, the strengthener of the two lands."

On the the right hand side, beginning from the foot, are the following scenes :—

I. The goddess Nut standing in a Persea tree, before the tomb of the deceased Nesi-pa-ur-shef, pouring out water from a vase  for his soul, which stands below drinking from its hands; behind kneels the deceased offering incense  to the goddess. The inscription which relates to this scene reads :—

ȧn Nut urt mest neteru

" *Behold Nut, mighty lady, genetrix of the gods* [*says she*],

seśep ḥetepu qebḥ qebḥ ȧb-k

Receive [*thou*] *offerings and cool water, may be refreshed heart thy*

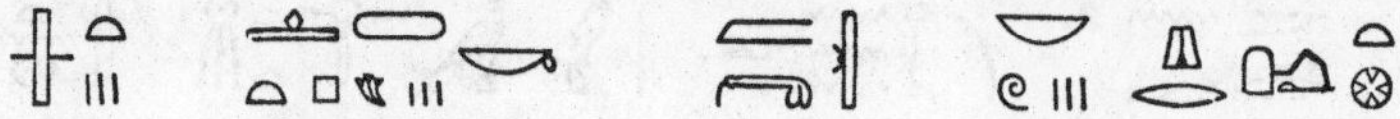

ȧmt ḥetepu - k embaḥ nebu χer-āba

with them. May be offerings thy in the presence of the lords of Cher-āba.

seqebḥ åb - k χer neha en nebt

May be refreshed heart thy under the sycamore of the lady of

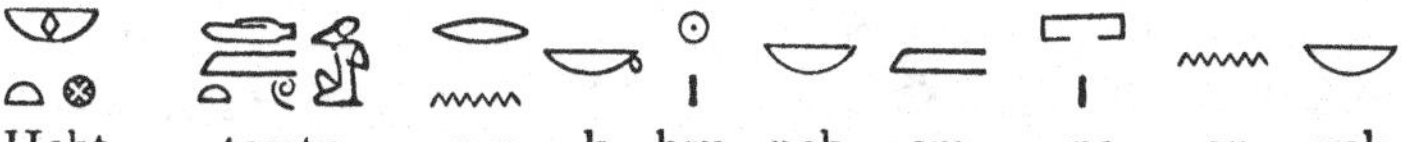

Ḥebt ṭemtu ren - k hru neb em pa en neb

Ḥebt, may be recited name thy day every in the house of the Lord

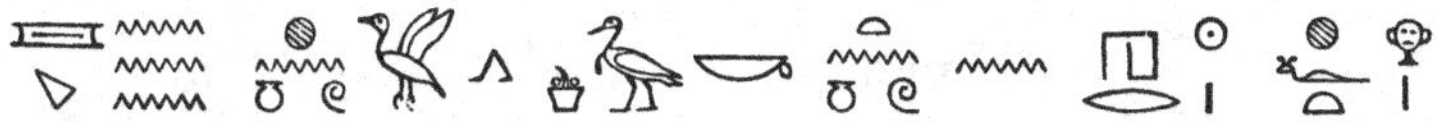

mer χennu ba - k tennu en hru χeft

of the Lake, may alight soul thy every day opposite

en Re - statet en Åusår åtf neterå en Åmen

Re - stau, Osiris, father divine of Åmen,

Nes - pa - ur - śef maātχeru

Nesi - pa - ur - shef triumphant"!

II. The deceased standing by the side of a table of offerings adoring the "mistress of Åmenta," who stands in a shrine holding a sceptre and a knife  in her left hand, and  *ānχ* in her right hand; she has two faces, one that of a lion, and the other that of a crocodile. The deceased says:—

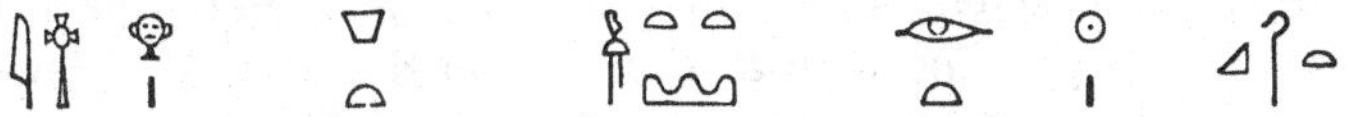

ånet' ḥrå ḥent Åmentet årit Rā ḥeqt

"*Hail to thee, mistress of the underworld, daughter of Rā, princess of*

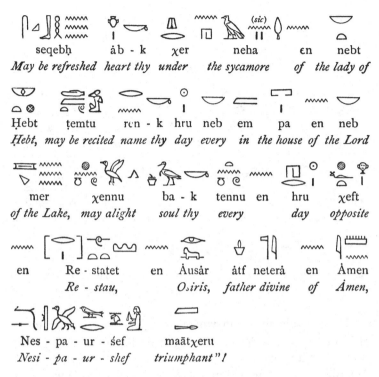

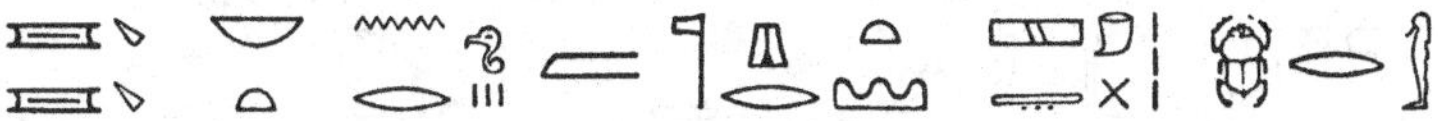

Ḥāt-ta[1] nebt neråu em Neter-χert śeta χeper

Ḥātta, lady of terrors in the underworld hidden, who art

[1] See Brugsch, *Dict. Géog.*, p. 273.

χenti ṭuat urt åru erma māχait

at the head of the underworld, mighty one, guardian near the balance

hru såp ḥāt ṭāt-s peri - å

on the day of testing hearts. May grant she that may come forth I

em maātχeru embaḥ uru em Neter-χert

with triumph in the presence of the mighty ones in the underworld,

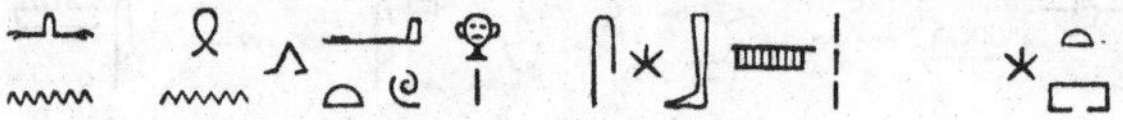

ån śenātu ḥer sebau ṭuat

not may be turned back I at the gates of the underworld."

III. Double shrine in which are seated the four children of Horus before tables of offerings; each god holds , and at his head is a winged *ut'at.* The two lines of inscription read, "O Mesθå, great god, lord of Åmenta, verily come, grant sepulchral meals of cakes, oxen, ducks, incense, libations, all things good and pure, all things good and pleasant, and an offering of *t'efa* food."[1]

IV. Scene in Åmenta. Rā, holding , and enthroned in a shrine in a boat, being rowed across the sky over the folds of the serpent of darkness, Āpepi, which Horus, "the avenger of his father, great god, lord of Åmenta,"[2] is piercing with a spear. Over the back of the boat

1 

2 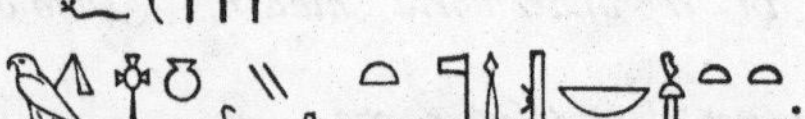

are seated, 1, the cynocephalus ape of Thoth , wearing
disk and crescent, 2, the god Shu , and 3, the god
Over the shrine is the winged disk . The deceased
stands adoring, and the inscription reads :—

Ȧusȧr[1] t'eṭ-f ȧnet' ḥrȧ-k neb neteru Ȧmen-Rā
Osiris, . . . says he, Hail to thee, lord of the gods, Ȧmen-Rā,

Ḥeru-χuti uben-k sep sen[2] pesṭ-k sep sen
Harmachis. Risest thou, risest thou, shinest thou, shinest thou,

χu-k nut-k nāi uȧa-k ṭā-k
makest splendid thou heaven thy, cometh boat thy, givest thou

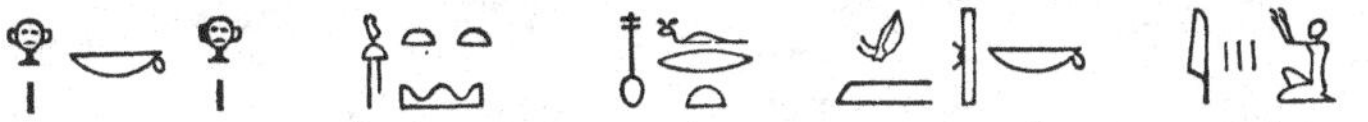

ḥrȧ-k ḥer Ȧmentet nefert setem-k ȧaiu
face thy over the underworld beautiful. Hearest thou the acclamations

en ȧmi-χet set ānχ ȧf-k ruṭ met-k
of those who follow after it. Lives flesh thy, germinates seed thy,

seq kesu-k renpȧ āt-k neteri ba-k
may be joined bones thy, may grow limbs thy, may be strong soul thy

śeps seχa (?)-k emsa χeft-k qeṭu uȧa-k
sacred, mayest thou . . . after enemies thy. The sailors of boat thy

[1] Here follow the usual titles of Nesi-pa-ur śef.

[2] *Sep sen*, lit. "time second," indicates that the words before it are to be repeated.

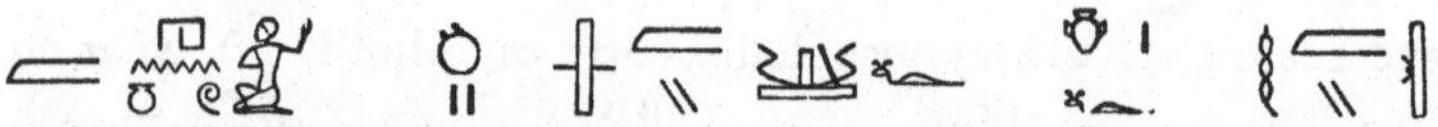

em hennu sep sen ȧmi uȧa - f ȧb-f net'emi
are rejoicing, rejoicing in boat his. Heart his rejoiceth

neb pet χnem-nef reś ur em
the lord of heaven. He joineth to himself joy, the mighty one in

ṭuat em ȧheh neter neb netert nebt ȧri
the underworld is in rejoicing. God every, goddess every, make

ȧaiu. en Ȧmen-Rā Ḥeru-χuti maa - ten su χāā-u
acclamations to Ȧmen-Rā Harmachis [when] see ye him diademed

em uȧa - f seχer - nef Āpep χer en Rā
in boat his. Overthrown has he Apepi, enemy of Rā,

χer en ser Nubθi em
has overthrown the flame in

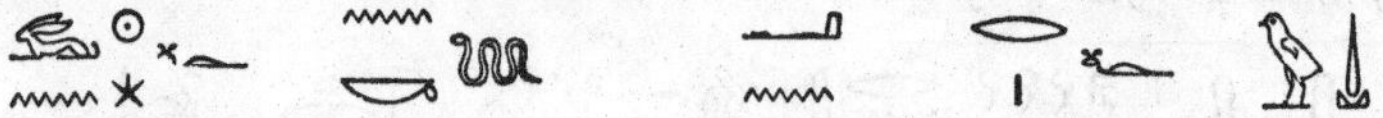

unnut-f Nek ān re - f ut'a
hour his, of Nek (the devil), turned back is mouth his, traverseth

Ȧmentet Re-stetet Ȧmen-Rā Ḥeru-χuti em
the underworld and Re-stau, Ȧmen-Rā Harmachis in

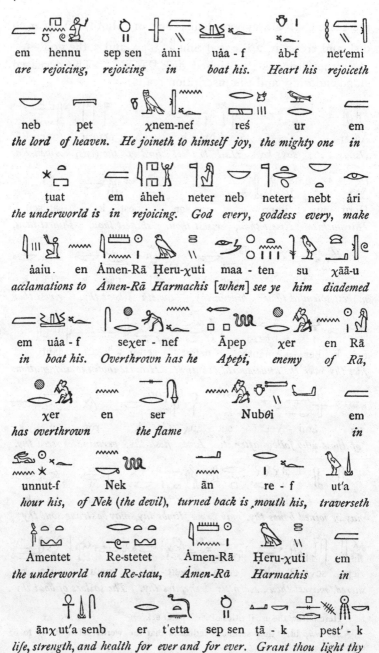

ānχ ut'a senb er t'etta sep sen ṭā - k pest' - k
life, strength, and health for ever and for ever. Grant thou light thy

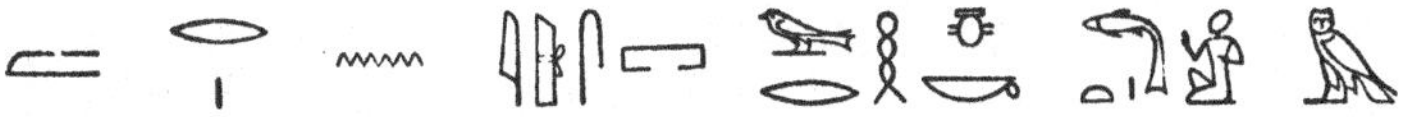

em re en àsi urḥ - k χat - à em

in the gate of the tomb, anoint thou body my with

ànnu - k Àusàr

colour (?) *thy, Osiris, Nesi-pa-ur-shef, triumphant!*

V. The goddess Nut separated from the embrace of the god Seb by "Shu, son of Rā, the great god, lord of Ma[nu]," [2] who stands beneath her with upraised hands and arms. The god Seb lies prostrate at his feet. On the right hand side of Shu are:—1, "the living soul of Osiris," [3] in the form of a man-headed hawk; 2, "the great god of Àmenta," ram-headed; and 3, Isis in the form of a winged serpent. On the left hand are also, 1, the "living soul of Osiris"; 2, the "great god of Àmenta," ram-headed; and 3, Nephthys in the form of a winged serpent. The inscription referring to the ram-headed god on the right reads:—  *neter pen ur em pet*, "this god (is) great in heaven"; that to the god on the left, 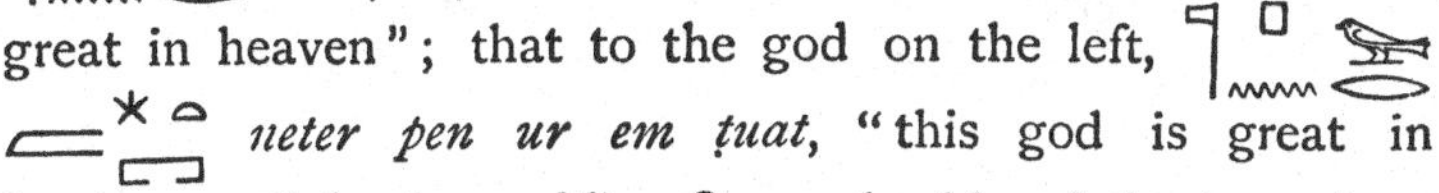 *neter pen ur em ṭuat*, "this god is great in in the *ṭuat*" (underworld). On each side of the bent form of the goddess are, 1, a ram  *ba en pet*, "the soul of heaven"; and 2, the deceased kneeling, with hands uplifted in adoration. To the right of this scene are two lines of inscription which read:—

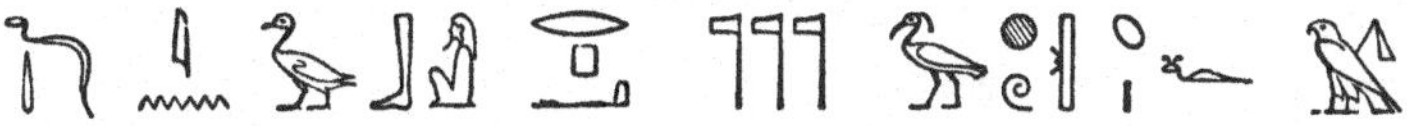

àn Seb erpā neteru χu se - f Ḥeru

Behold Seb, prince of the gods glorifying son his Horus,

[1] I have omitted the titles.

[2] 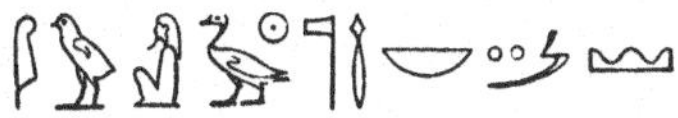

[3] 

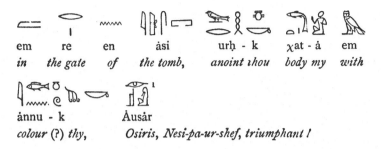

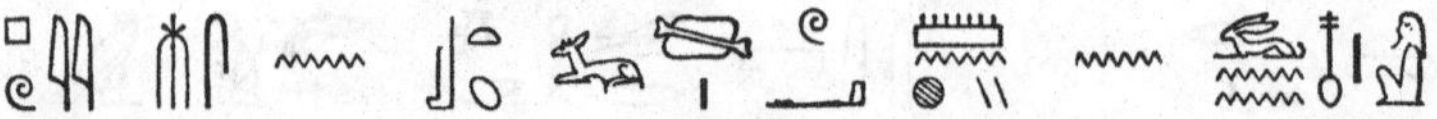

pui mes en Åuset uāuā menχi en Unnefer
this, born of Isis, heir perfect of Unnefer.

ṭā - sen tat en χat - å nefu en fent-å
May give they bread for body my, air for nostril my,

neter sentrå er śen - å
incense for body my !

VI. Thoth, ibis-headed, "lord of divine words, veritable scribe of the cycle of the gods," standing in a shrine, by the side of a table of offerings, holding ☥ in his hands. To the right are two lines of inscription which read:—

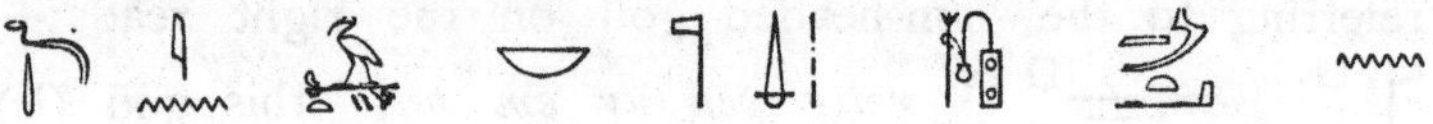

ån Teḥuti neb neter t'et ān maāt en
Behold Thoth, lord of divine words, scribe veritable of

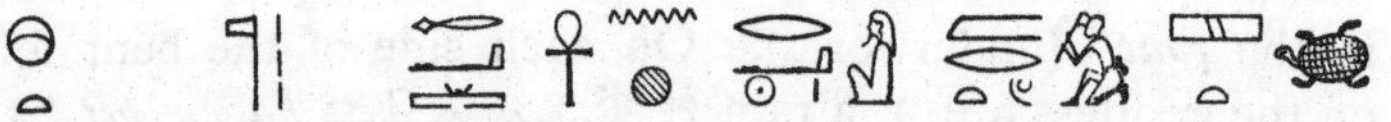

paut neteru āā ānχ Rā mertu śet
the cycle of the gods great, lives Rā, dies the tortoise,

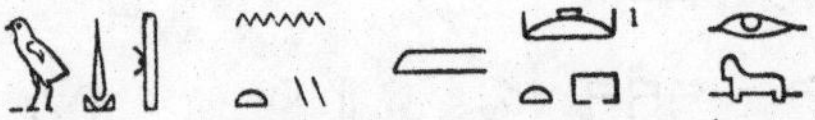

ut'a enti em[1] aat Åusår
is strong he that is in the coffin, Osiris, Nesi-pa-ur-shef, triumphant.

VII. Deceased offering incense, and pouring out libations before the god Osiris, seated in a shrine; behind the god stands Isis.

[1] Coffin has 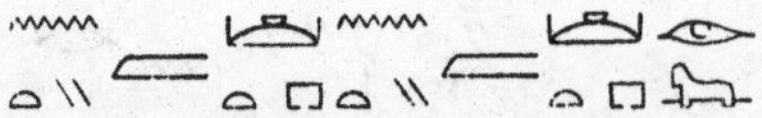

On the left hand side, beginning at the head, are the following scenes:—

I. Deceased offering incense and libation by the side of a table of offerings. Thoth, "lord of law," ibis-headed, and Isis with outstretched wings, standing one on each side of a standard , with disk and plumes, emblem of "Osiris, lord of eternity."

II. Thoth, ibis-headed, wearing , and holding by the side of a table of offerings. To the left two lines of inscription, duplicate of that on the right side, scene VI.

III. Osiris seated. To the right of him Isis, Nephthys, Shu and Ḥeka ; the first three of these gods have in the right hand, the fourth has a staff in the form of a serpent. To the left of Osiris are Thoth and Horus. Beneath these gods is a serpent, part of the body of which is erect on the left hand side. Beneath the serpent is a throne with steps on each side ; one side is ornamented with the sun's disk shedding rays of light , , , and . On it is also inscribed *pa nefer*, "the beautiful house." To the right of the throne is a crocodile-headed quadruped with horns, called *neb ṭuat Renenet*, "Renenet, lady of the underworld"; to the left is a similar animal called *neb ṭuat Shanai*, "Shanai, lord of the underworld." Further to the left is a serpent-headed god holding a knife in each hand, and above is inscribed .

The inscription of the two lines reads:—

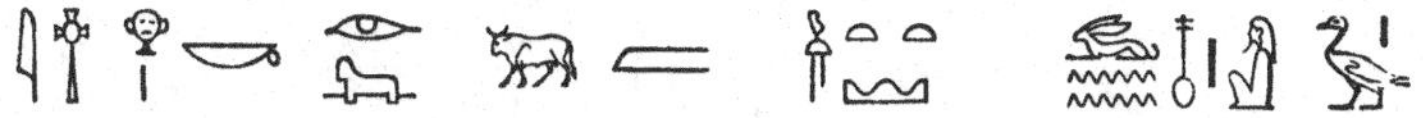

ȧnet'	ḥrȧ-k	Ȧusȧr	ka	em	Ȧmentet	Un-nefer	se
Hail	*to thee,*	*Osiris,*	*bull*	*of*	*the underworld,*	*Unnefer,*	*son of*

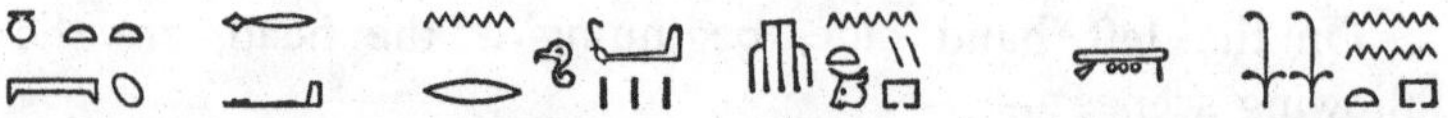

Nut, āa nerȧu χenti ta enenet

Nut, mighty one of terrors at the head of the land of rest (?),

uā neteri ḥer ȧb er ta ur ṭuat - tu

only one, mighty one, within ....

IV. The scene of the weighing of the heart against Law in a balance. On the support of the balance sits a cynocephalus ape, the index is held in one hand of Anubis, and the chains to which the pans are attached, in the other. The chains are formed of links made of *ṭeṭ* and *sa* ; the emblem of stability represents Osiris, and the buckle, Isis. Under the right arm of the balance kneels the deceased, "Nesi-Ȧmen, triumphant"! receiving his heart in his left hand, and his two eyes in the right; above him is a rectangular man-headed object which is described as , "Maāt, mistress of Amenta." To the right of the balance stand the deceased, having on his head, and in each of his upraised hands; a *maāt*-headed figure with one upraised arm and hand; "Ȧmentet, mistress of the house of life"; the goddess Maāt holding deceased by the hand, and two tables of offerings. To the left of the balance is Thoth recording the result of the weighing; Horus "the avenger of his father, great god;" the beast Amemit (*i.e.*, devourer), part hippopotamus, part lion, and part crocodile; all these stand before Osiris seated in a shrine accompanied by Isis. The speech of Thoth is as follows:—

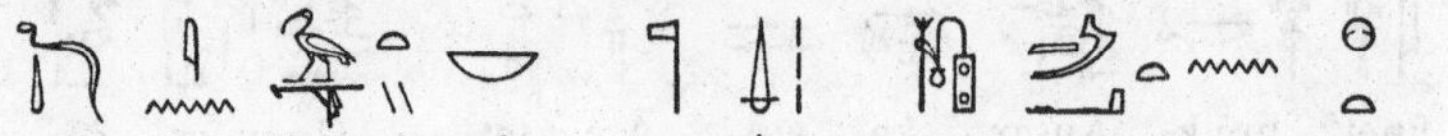

ȧn Teḥuti neb neter t'eṭu ān maāt en paut

Behold Thoth, lord of divine words, scribe of law of the cycle

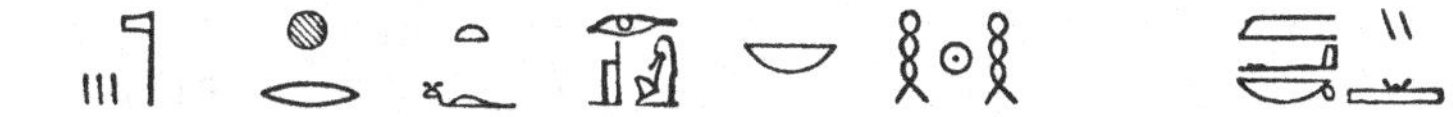

neteru χer tef Ȧusȧr neb ḥeḥ māki

of the gods, before father Osiris, lord of eternity [*says he*], " *Verily*

Ȧusȧr ȧtef neterȧ en Ȧmen Nesi - pa - ur - śef maātχeru

Osiris, father divine of Ȧmen, Nesi - pa - ur - shef, triumphant

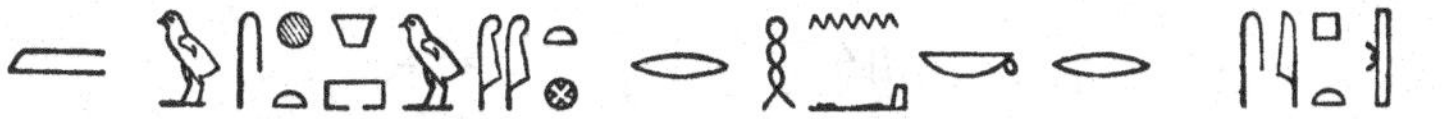

em useχt Maāt er ḥenā - k er sȧpt

in the hall of double law is with thee for the trying of

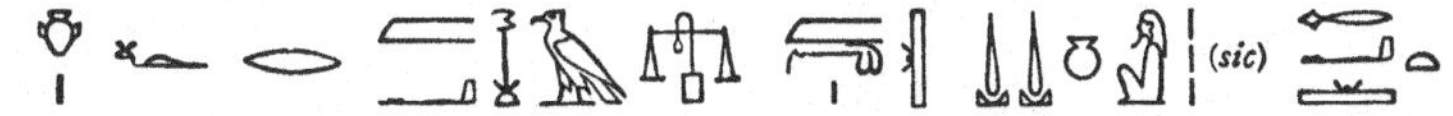

ȧb - f er māχa embaḥ t'at'anut āāt

heart his in the balance before the divine chiefs mighty,

nebu ṭuat su qem maāti ȧn

the lords of the underworld. He is found right and true, not

qemtu seχef neb nu ta ȧb - f per

is found defect any of earth [*in*] *heart his, he comes forth*

em maātχeru em useχt Neterχert ṭāṭā - nef ȧb - f

in triumph from the hall of the underworld. Gives to him heart his

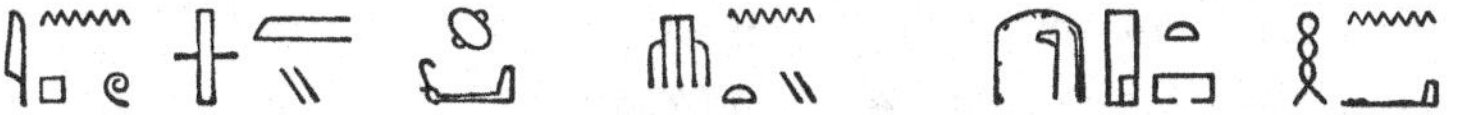

Ȧnpu ȧmi ut χenti neter ḥet ḥenā

Anubis in the coffin, at the head of the divine house, and

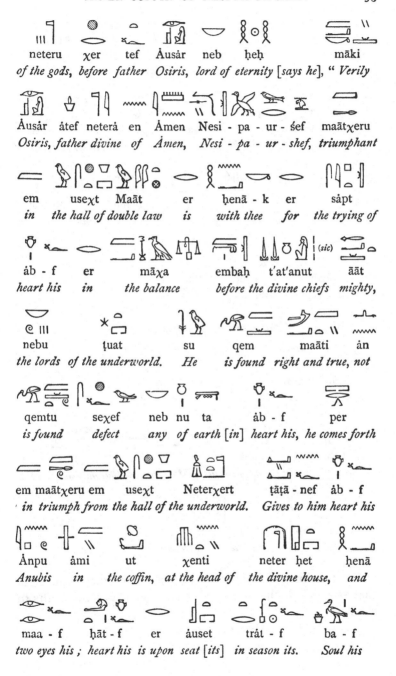

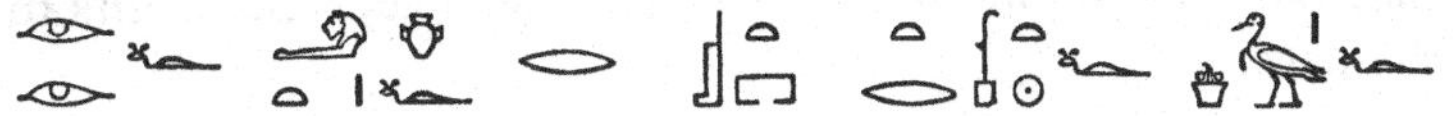

maa - f ḥāt - f er ȧuset trȧt - f ba - f

two eyes his ; heart his is upon seat [*its*] *in season its. Soul his*

er pet χat - f er ṭuat mȧ śesi
is in heaven, body his is in the underworld, like the followers of

Ḥeru ȧmmā χat - f ṭāṭā Ȧnpu ȧmi χent
Horus. Grant that body his may place Anubis in the innermost part of

en pa nefer ȧmmā-nef ḥetep em Re-statet
the beautiful house, may be given to him offerings in Re - stau,

embaḥ Unnefer t'etta
in the presence of Unnefer, for ever"!

The inscription relating to Osiris reads:—

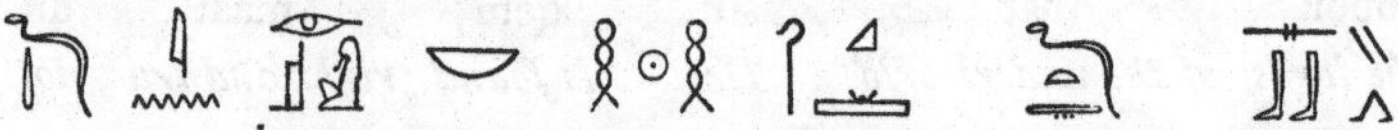

ȧn Ȧusȧr neb ḥeḥ ḥeq t'etta sebebi
Behold Osiris, lord of eternity, prince of everlasting, traversing

ḥeḥ em āḥā - f ṭāt - f per - ȧ
myriads of years in period of life his, "May grant he that may come forth I

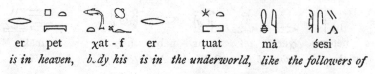

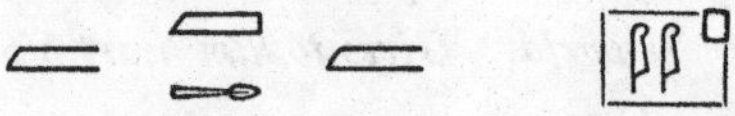

em maātχeru em useχt maāt
with triumph in the hall of double law."

The two lines of inscription to the left of the shrine state that Isis and Nephthys will give the usual sepulchral gifts to the deceased.

V. Shrine in which stand Anubis (?) jackal-headed, Osiris ram-headed, and Isis lion-headed.

VI. The entrance to the tomb of the deceased in the Theban mountain, above which the soul of the deceased is seated. From the mountain comes forth the goddess Hathor in the form of a cow, wearing disk and plumes, and a Hathor-headed *ānχ* round the neck. The inscription reads  *χeft neb-set*, "opposite her lord." Beneath is "Anubis, great god, lord of Amenta," jackal-headed, wearing . The scene is filled up by winged serpents,  and O.

On the foot of the coffin are painted the goddess Nephthys with upraised arms, from which hang 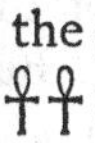; the four children of Horus, Mesθȧ, Ḥāpi, Ṭuamāutef, and Qebḥsennuf; the goddess Ȧmentet, and a serpent-headed deity. The inscriptions at the extreme end of each side state that Isis and Nephthys will grant to the deceased the usual sepulchral offerings. Length, 6ft 1½in.; width at shoulders, 1ft. 9in.; at foot, 1ft. 1½in.

VI. *Outer Coffin of Nesi-pa-ur-shef.*

(Description of the Outside.)[1]

This coffin, like that which was placed inside it, is made in the shape of a mummy; the head-dress is painted green, the face yellow, the hands are crossed over the breast, and the inscriptions and scenes upon it are painted in light and dark green, yellow, and red upon a white ground. The beard is wanting, as also are the objects which were originally held in the hands. The cover was fixed to the coffin by means of eight dowels into which pegs of wood were driven. The scenes upon it are painted on a larger scale, and with the inscriptions are substantially the same as those found on the inner coffin. The necklace is of the same pattern, the arms and wrists are ornamented in the same way; the arrangement of the scenes is the same, but many details are here omitted. Beneath the figure of Nut with outstretched wings are three lines of inscription, but large parts of them are effaced. The two scenes on the projecting foot of the cover

[1] N.B. The inside of the cover is neither painted nor inscribed.

lack the inscriptions which accompany the same scenes on the cover of the inner coffin. The inscriptions on the other parts of the cover, which are identical with those on the inner coffin, are not repeated here.

Around the outside edge of the coffin are two lines of inscription which contain the same text as those on the edge of the inner coffin. The scenes painted on the outside, beginning at the foot on the right hand side, are as follows:—

I. The tomb of the deceased in the Theban mountains and *tets* ; on the top is written  *Ȧusȧr*, "Osiris," Hathor in form of a cow, winged serpent (Isis), Anubis, the goddess Maāt, and standard ; before these stands the deceased offering a vessel  and , incense.

II. Deceased in a shrine standing by the side of a table of offerings, making an offering of 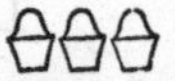 to Mesθȧ, Ḥāpi, Ṭuamāutef, and Qebḥsennuf, the four children of Horus.

III. The goddess Nut raised from the embrace of Seb by Shu; on each side is the soul of the deceased by the side of a table of offerings.

IV. Thoth in a shrine.

V. Osiris, ram-headed, with horns and uræus. The deceased in a shrine offers incense to him.

VI. Nephthys standing with upraised hands and arms, and double .

VII. Standard, with plumes and disk, emblem of Osiris, the goddess Isis and the deceased offering 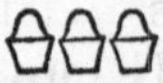.

VIII. Thoth, ibis-headed, adoring Osiris, seated, behind whom stand Isis and Nephthys; serpent and serpent-headed god who holds a knife  in each hand; throne, with steps on each side, ornamented with  and .

IX. The goddess Maāt, the god Cheperȧ, Rā, ram-headed, and the god Ḥeka in the boat of the Sun sailing across the sky. Beneath the mummy of the deceased, upon which fall rays of light, are disks and stars  proceeding from an inverted head of the hawk of Horus. To the right are offerings, uræus and stand, and a hawk-headed god; to the left are offerings, a vulture, and a bearded man-headed god. The deceased stands by the side of a table of offerings and says:—

ȧnet' ḥrȧ-k Rā Ḥeru-χuti Temu ka ḥer ȧb Ȧnnu
Hail to thee, Rā Harmachis Atmu, bull within Heliopolis!

uben - k sep sen pesṭ - k sep sen χuu - k
Risest thou, risest thou, shinest thou, shinest thou, glorious art thou,

χii - k nāi uȧa - k ṭā - k pesṭ - k em
splendid art thou coming in boat thy! Cast thou radiance thy in

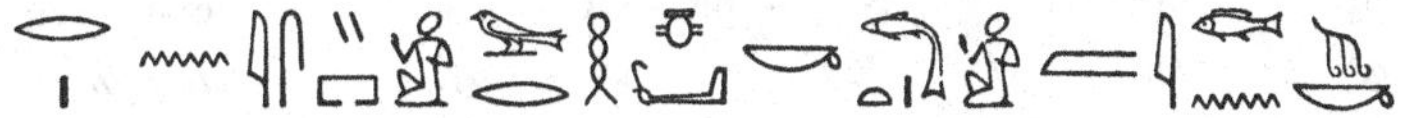

re en ȧsi - ȧ urḥ - k χat - ȧ em ȧnnu - k
the door of tomb my, anoint thou body my with colour (?) thy,

Ȧusȧr Nesi - pa - ur - śef maātχeru
Osiris, Nesi - pa - ur - shef, triumphant!

X. Horus leading the deceased into the presence of Osiris, behind whom stands Isis.

XI. The goddess Nephthys holding ☥ in her upraised arms and.

Inside, on the bottom of the outer coffin, is painted on a purple ground a figure of the god Osiris in the form of with human face and arms and hands, holding and ;

on the top of it are plumes and a disk. The perpendicular line of inscription reads:—

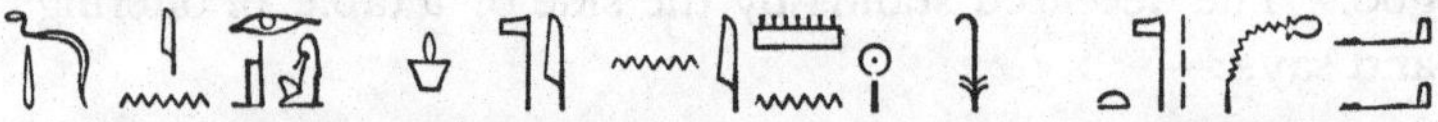

ȧn Ȧusȧr ȧtef neterȧ en Ȧmen-Rā suten neteru āb
Behold Osiris, father divine of Amen-Rā, king of the gods, priest

ḥer ȧri neter sentrȧ neb ī em ȧuset - f neb
making offerings of incense all, coming into place his every,

sāb em ȧuset urt ḥer ān neter ḥet
councillor in the place mighty, president of the scribes of the divine house

en Ȧmen-pa Nesi - pa - ur - śef maāt*χ*eru
of the Ȧmen temple, Nesi - pa - ur - shef, triumphant!

4. Coffins of Pa-kepu, a Water-carrier at Thebes, about B.C. 500.

I. *The Outer Coffin.*

The painted wooden coffins of Pa-kepu were presented to the Fitzwilliam Museum by H.R.H. the Prince of Wales, in 1869. The outer coffin is 6 ft. 10 in. long, and the inner is 5 ft. 11 in. They are well made and strong, but the artist's work is poor.

The face is red, the beard is black, and the head-dress is painted with stripes of red and black, upon a yellow ground; the scenes on the cover are in green, black, purple, yellow and drab, and the inscriptions, arranged in short lines, are painted in black upon a white and yellow ground alternately.

The scenes painted below the necklace on the outside of the cover are as follows:—

I. Winged disk with uræi; by the side of each wing 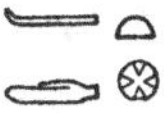 *Beḥuṭet.*

II. The heart of the deceased being weighed against Maāt ; Thoth leading the deceased into the presence of Horus and Osiris; the four children of Horus standing upon a lotus flower; Isis, Nephthys, Mesθȧ, Hāpi, Ṭuamāutef, Qebḥsennuf, two crocodile-headed gods, Horus and Thoth; these last four gods represent some of the forty-two "assessors."

III. Inscription, which reads[1]:—"May Osiris at the head of the underworld, great god, lord of Abydos, grant a royal offering; thousands of cakes, thousands of jugs of beer thousands of oxen, thousands of ducks, thousands of incense thousands of linen bandages, thousands of vessels of oil, thousands of vessels of wine, thousands of vessels of milk, thousands of offerings, thousands of offerings of *t'efau* food, thousands of all beautiful and pure things to the *ka* of Osiris, the water-carrier of the western part of Thebes."

IV. Mummy of the deceased lying on a bier, beneath which are the four Canopic jars containing his intestines; Anubis stands by the bier giving  *ānχ* "life" to the mummy; on each side is a hawk wearing a disk. The inscriptions read, "Beḥuṭet, great god, lord of heaven, Shu, may he grant all offerings of *t'efa* food and things," "Beḥuṭet,

1 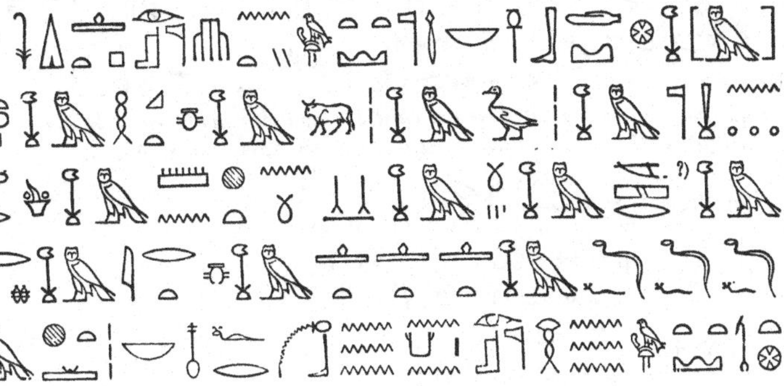

great god, lord of heaven, may he grant offerings of *t'efa* food."[1]

V. An inscription which repeats the entreaty for sepulchral meals for[2] "the *ka* of Osiris, the water-carrier of the Western part of Thebes, this Pa-kepu, triumphant, lord of watchful adoration, son of Ȧmen-ḥetep-ȧu-ȧnt, born of the lady of the house, this Āȧrru, triumphant."

VI. Standard, in the form of a lotus flower, having *menȧts* , disk, plumes and uræi; hawk of Horus and *ut'at.* To the right are Mesθȧ and Qebḥsennuf, to the left Hāpi and Ṭuamāutef. The inscriptions are identical with those above.

VII. Repetition of inscription asking for sepulchral meals.

VIII. Rā, Cheperȧ, Thoth and two other gods sailing across the sky in a boat. Before and behind the boat are  and a cynocephalus ape  in adoration.

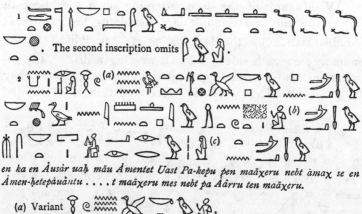

IX. On the projecting foot of the coffin are *ut'at* and hawk of Horus wearing disk and  in a shrine. The inscriptions on each side ask for sepulchral foods.

1 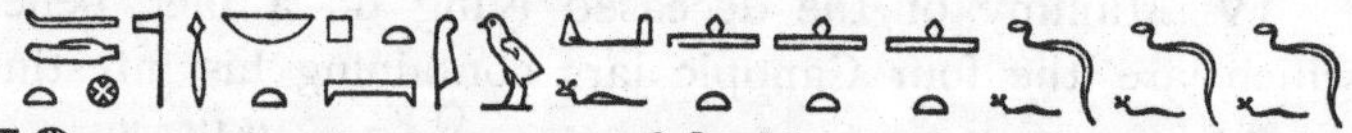
. The second inscription omits .

2 
en ka en Ȧusȧr uaḥ māu Ȧmentet Uast Pa-kepu ṗen maāχeru nebt ȧmaχ se en Ȧmen-ḥetepȧuȧntu . . . . t maāχeru mes nebt pa Āȧrru ten maāχeru.

(*a*) Variant .

(*b*) Variant .

(*c*) Variant .

The inside of the cover is blank; it was fastened to the coffin by means of eight dowels.

On the bottom of the coffin inside are painted: 1, The goddess Nut, standing in a persea tree pouring out water for the soul of the deceased, which stands beneath drinking it from its hands; 2, three lines of inscription in which Osiris is entreated to grant sepulchral meals to the deceased; 3, serpent, on the neck of which is ; and 4, Horus (?), standing wearing crown and plumes, and holding in his hands the crook , whip, , and sceptre . On the rounded end of the coffin are , on the right hand side is Nephthys standing on , on the left is Isis standing on , and on the foot .

On the outside of the coffin, between yellow and red lines, is a line of inscription, painted in green upon a white ground, which reads :—

suten ṭā ḥetep Rā Ḥeru-χuti ḥer neteru per

Give a royal oblation Rā Harmachis, chief of the gods coming forth

em χut Tem neb ta Ȧnnu Ptaḥ - seker -

from the horizon, Ȧtmu, lord of the land of Heliopolis, Ptaḥ - Seker -

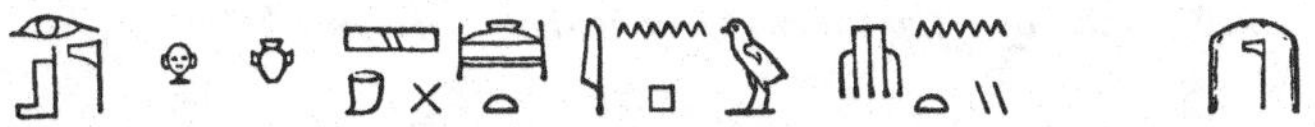

Ȧusȧr ḥer ȧb śetat Ȧnpu χenti neter saḥ

Ȧusȧr within the tomb, Ȧnubis at the head of the divine hall,

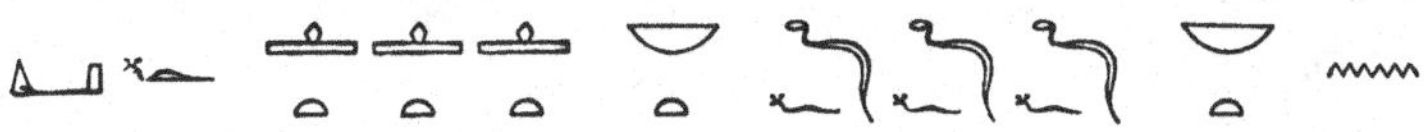

ṭā - f ḥetepu nebt t'efau nebt en

may give he offerings all, t'efau *food all, to*

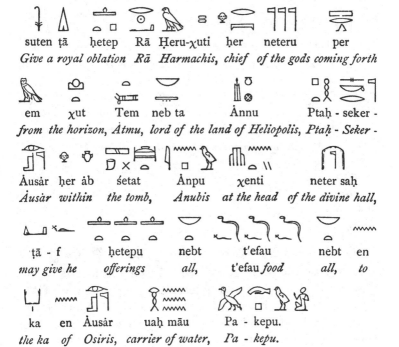

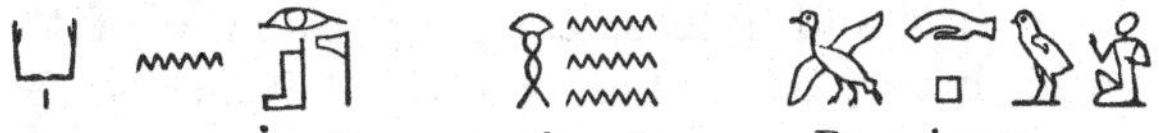

ka en Ȧusȧr uaḥ māu Pa - kepu.

the ka of Osiris, carrier of water, Pa - kepu.

The inner coffin, measuring 5 ft. 11 in. in length, which contains the mummy, has upon it the greater number of the scenes which are painted upon the outer coffin. The few inscriptions on the cover are of no interest, and the scenes are, if anything, more rudely drawn; the method of ornamentation is the same. On the outside of the coffin are two perpendicular lines of inscription which read:—

I. 

Ha Ȧusȧr uaḥ māu ḥer Ȧmentet Uast

"*Hail, Osiris, carrier of water over the west of Thebes,*

pa - kep maāχeru mes Ȧrru

Pa - kep, triumphant, born of Ȧrru."

II. 

Ha Ȧusȧr uaḥ māu ḥer Ȧmentet Uast

"*Hail, Osiris, carrier of water over the west of Thebes,*

pa - kep se uaḥ māu Ȧmen - ḥetep - īt

Pa - kep, son of the carrier of water Ȧmen - ḥetep - īt,

maāχeru

triumphant."

On the head are disk of the sun ⊙, beetle, *śen*, and emblems of the west, and east; on the foot is a bull (Osiris), wearing disk and uræus, carrying mummy of the deceased upon his back; before him is a vessel of incense. The pedestal at the back of the coffin has the emblem of stability painted upon it.

5. Mummy and Coffin of a Person unknown.

Mummy, of a late period, enclosed in a *cartonnage* case, the greater part of which has disappeared ; the cover of the coffin in which it was placed is also wanting. The pectoral, parts of which still remain, has painted upon it a scene in which the deceased is represented lying on a bier, beneath which are the four jars which contained the intestines of the deceased. The god of the dead, Anubis, stands by the side of the bier, and Isis and Nephthys stand at the head and foot respectively. Lower down, to the right, are two of the children of Horus, Isis, and Anubis, jackal-headed, with his whip , seated on the tomb  ; to the left are the other two children of Horus, Nephthys, and Anubis as before. Between two perpendicular rows of gods is a line of inscription which runs :—

I am unable to read any more than the first few words, and it is tolerably clear that the writer either copied a text which he could not read, or that he invented what is here written. The mummy appears to belong to the very late Roman period about A.D. 350, and it is probable that the coffin in which it now lies once belonged to some one else.

Presented to the Museum by the Hon. George Townshend.[1]

Canopic Jars.

6—9. Set of canopic jars made for "the lady of the house," Shepset-Àment, daughter of Nes-pa-qa-Shuti. The inscriptions on each are inlaid in blue, and the , which is over each inscription, in dark sage-green colour.

[1] See Middleton (Conyers), *Miscellaneous Works*, London, 1752, Vol. IV., p. 170, ff., and Blumenbach, J. F., *Decas Collectionis suae Craniorum diversarum Gentium Illustrata*, p. 13. Gottingae, 1790.

6. Calcareous stone jar, for holding intestines, with cover in the form of a man's head to represent Mesthȧ; the face is painted yellow. On the front of the jar is inscribed :—

1. 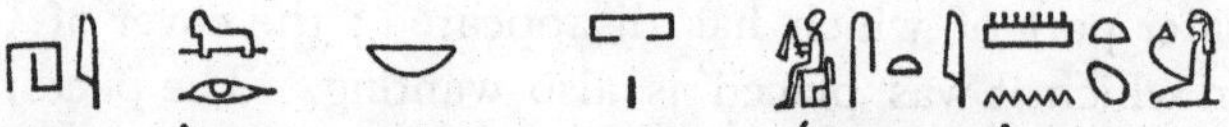

Hȧ Åusȧr nebt pa Śepset - Åment

Hail, Osiris, lady of the house, Shepset - Åment,

2. 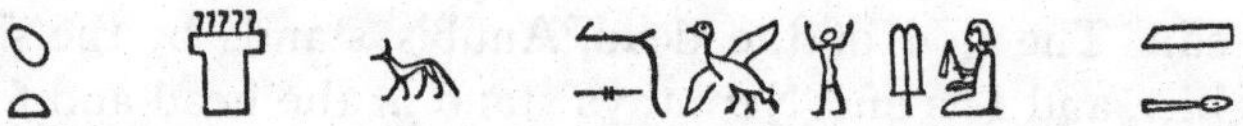

set sa sāb Nes - pa - qa - śuti maātχeru

daughter of the councillor, Nes - pa - qa - shuti, triumphant!

3. 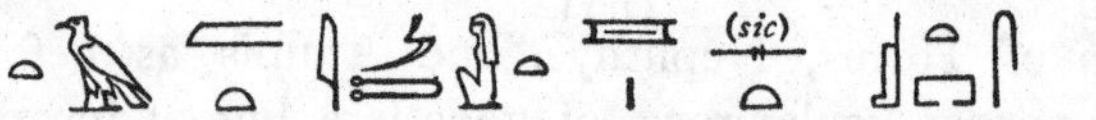

ta . . . . meri set åuset-s

Fashioneth thee he that loveth thee; may her place be

4. 

em ḥet - θ ḥer ȧrit ḥennu θes

in house thy to make completion and resurrection.

16 in. high.

7. Calcareous stone jar, for holding intestines, with cover in the form of a dog's head to represent Ḥāpi; on the front of the jar is inscribed :—

1. 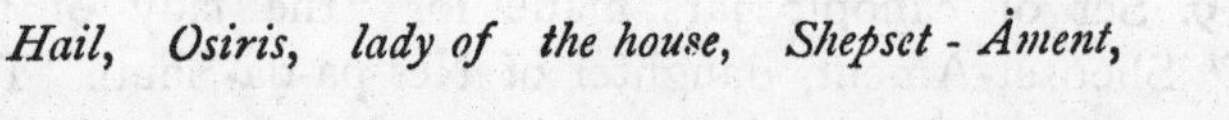

Hȧ Åusȧr neb pa Śepset - Åment

Hail, Osiris, lady of the house, Shepset - Åment,

2. 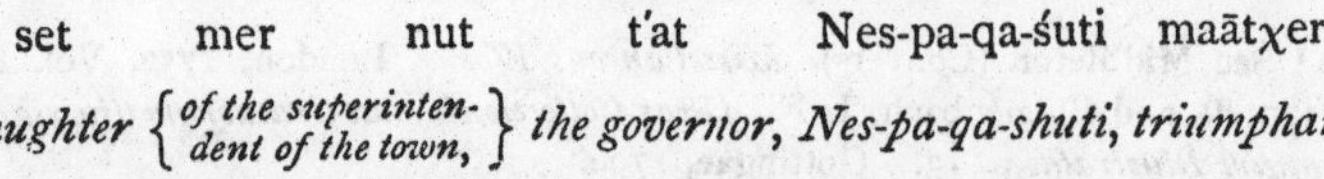

set mer nut t'at Nes-pa-qa-śuti maātχeru

daughter {*of the superintendent of the town,*} *the governor, Nes-pa-qa-shuti, triumphant!*

3. 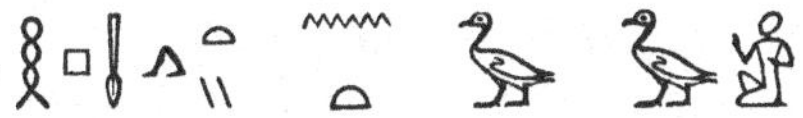

ḥep · ti net se se - å

Runneth to thee .... daughter my (?)

4. 

er åuset - f åm - t ḥer sam χat enti ....

upon seat its in thee to unite bodies of ....

17 in. high.

8. Calcareous stone jar, for holding intestines, with cover in the form of a jackal's head, to represent Ṭuamāutef; on the front of the jar is inscribed :—

1. 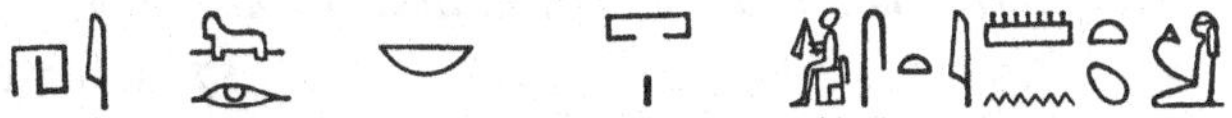

Hå Åusår neb pa Śepset Åment

Hail, Osiris, lady of the house, Shepset - Åment,

2. 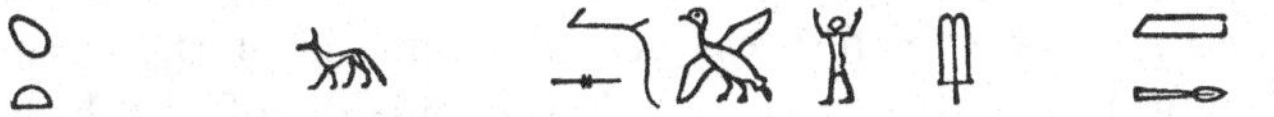

set sāb Nes - pa - qa - śuti maātχeru

daughter of the councillor, Nes - pa - qa - shuti, triumphant!

3. 

ṭua - māut - f en Rā ḥer-t

.... *Rā over thee,*

4. 

ḥer tem åb - f åm-t en t'etta

that may not depart he from thee for ever.

16½ in. high.

9. Calcareous stone jar for holding intestines, with cover in the form of a hawk's head to represent Qebḥsennuf; on the front of the jar is inscribed :—

1. 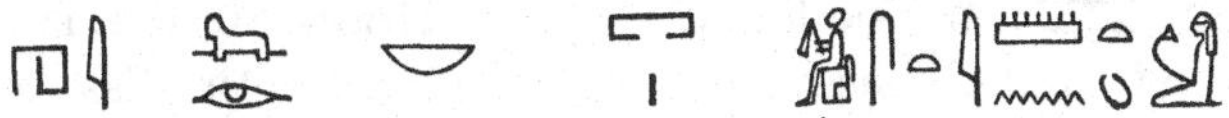

Hå Åusår neb pa Śepset - Åment

Hail, Osiris, lady of the house, Shepset - Åment,

2. 

set mer nut t'at Nes-pa-qa-śuti maātχeru

daughter {*of the superintendent of the town*} *the governor, Nes-pa-qa-shuti, triumphant!*

3. 

iu net Qebḥ-sennu-f bāḥ

Comes to thee Qebḥsennuf, overflowing

4. 

em qebḥ ḥer āuḥ mā - f hru neb

with cool water, to scatter abroad libations his day every

17 in. high.

Boxes for Holding Ushabtiu Figures.

10. Rectangular wooden box, with raised rounded ends, for holding *ushabtiu* figures. On the outside of the cover is painted a boat , and round the outside of the box is written:—

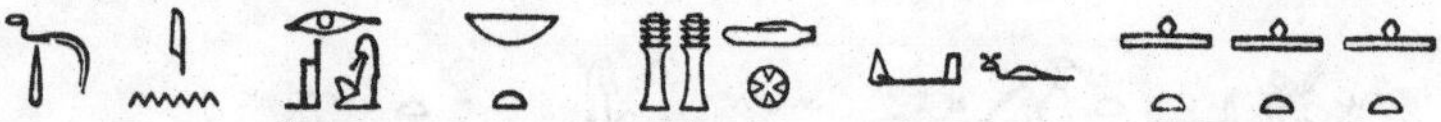

ȧn Ȧusȧr nebt Ṭeṭṭeṭ ṭā - f ḥetep

" *Behold Osiris, lord of Tattu, may give he offerings*

nebt t'efau neb en Ȧusȧr Pa - χreṭ - er - āā maātχeru

all, tchefau *food all to Osiris, Pa - chrat - er - āā, triumphant."*

The sides of the box are kept together by wooden pegs.

Thebes, XIXth dynasty. $11\frac{1}{2}$ in. × 11 in. × $6\frac{1}{4}$ in.

11. Rectangular wooden box, in the form of a shrine , on the sides of which are painted:—1. The doors of the tomb with bolts ; 2. The four children of Horus, Mesthȧ, Ḥāpi, Ṭuamāutef, and Qebḥsennuf; 3. Standard, with disk and plumes, emblems of Osiris, and Isis and Nephthys in the form of uræi; and 4. Two bearded men and two snake-headed gods. The figures are painted green and red upon a yellow ground. The sixteen small green glazed faïence *ushabtiu* figures which are in it do not belong to the box. Each figure is 3¾ in. high, and is inscribed with one line of hieroglyphics which read :  *Ausár Nesi-χensu-pa maātχeru*, "Osiris, Nesi-Chensu-pa-[chreṭ], triumphant." Fifteen of the figures have both hands crossed over the breast, and one has the left hand only laid on the breast, while the right arm hangs straight by his side. A variant of the name which occurs is . In the bottom of the box are some fragments of a papyrus and the linen in which it was wrapped ; the few traces of characters which remain on one of the pieces show that it was written during the Ptolemaic period.

Thebes, XIXth dynasty. 15½ in. × 9½ in.

12. Rectangular wooden box, in the form of a shrine , on the sides of which are painted: 1. The doors of the tomb with bolts ; 2. Five bearded man-headed gods, each holding a knife  in his hand; 3. *ṭeṭ*, having horns, disk and plumes , emblem of Osiris, and Isis , and Nephthys , in the form of serpents. Over the side on which doors of the tomb are painted are three winged disks with pendent uræi, and over the other three sides is a design composed of buckles and *ṭeṭs* .

Thebes, XIXth dynasty. 15½ in. × 9 in. (at base).

13. Uninscribed rectangular wooden box, with raised, rounded wooden ends; the inside and outside are covered with a thin layer of plaster. Thebes. 8¼ in. × 4¼ in. × 4¼ in.

(Presented by the late Rev. Greville J. Chester, B.A.)

14. Sepulchral wooden box, in the shape of a tomb, for holding *ushabtiu* figures, on the cover of which is inscribed in Demotic the name of the person for whom it was made. The wooden hawk which now surmounts it belongs to another box. On the sides are painted: 1. Two figures of

Anubis, standing at the doors of the tomb, and three seated figures. 2. and figures of Àmseth and Ḥāpi. 3. and figure of ṭeṭ, having on the top plumes and horns, and on each side an uræus; that on the right wears the white crown, that on the left wears the red crown. 4. and figures of Qebḥsennuf and Ṭuāmāutef. The inscriptions are as follows:—

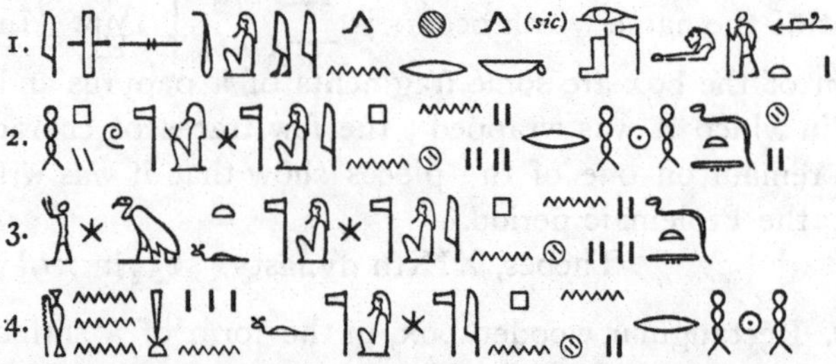

The name of the man for whom the box appears to have been made seems to occur in line 1: Ḥā-ser-uāt. The hieroglyphic legends are of an unusual nature, and are very roughly written.

(Presented by the late H. B. Brady, Esq.)

PTAḤ-SEKER-ÀUSÀR FIGURE.

15. Ptaḥ-Seker-Osiris figure, man-headed, wearing horns, disk, and plumes; the face is painted yellow, the head-dress blue, and the breastplate red and black upon a yellow and white ground. The figure is fastened into a rectangular stand, and is inscribed:—

suten ṭā ḥetep en Àusàr χentet Àmentet neter āa neb Àbṭu ṭā-f perχeru àh apṭ en Àusàr Neb-se-à-merts set ut'eb t'eχ mes àḥet . . . . .

The front of the stand is ornamented with  and each side with a design . In the stand, in front of the figure, is a rectangular cavity, in which was placed a portion of one of the intestines of the deceased, mummified, and wrapped in linen bandages. The cavity was closed by a wooden cover, sealed with wax, on the top of which was a wooden figure of the hawk of Horus wearing a disk; the hawk faced the figure of the god.

Aḥmîm, about B.C. 400. 23½ in. high.

USHABTIU FIGURES.

16. White limestone *ushabti* figure, with hands crossed over the breast; the face is painted red, the eyebrows and eyelashes black, and the head-dress blue with yellow stripes. It was made for  Åmen-em-uȧa, and is inscribed in hieratic with a version of the 6th chapter of the Book of the Dead in six perpendicular lines.

Thebes. Height, 9¾ in.

17. White limestone *ushabti* figure of Sen-net'em, an officer in the "seat of law," with hands crossed over the breast; the face is painted red, the eyebrows and eyelashes black, and the head-dress green. In the right hand is a plough , in the left a whip  and rope sack. The figure is inscribed with six lines of hieroglyphics in black, which contain a version of the 6th chapter of the Book of the Dead. They read :—

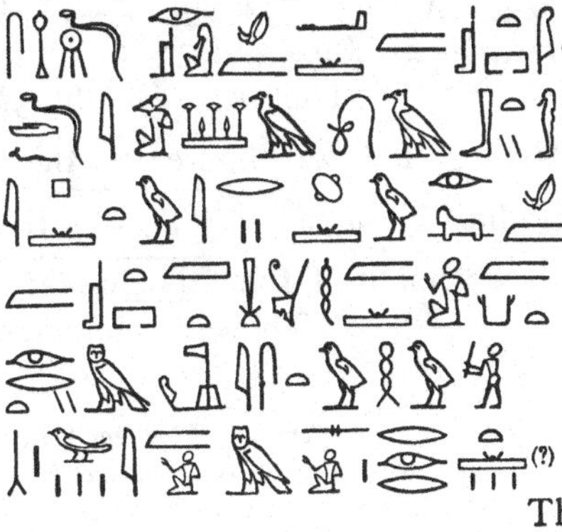

Thebes. Height, 9 in.

18. White limestone *ushabti* figure of Mesu; the face is red, the head-dress black, and the hands are crossed over the breast. The inscription is  *Ȧusȧr Mesu*, "Osiris Mesu." Thebes. Height, 5¾ in.

19. Blue glazed faïence *ushabti* figure of Pi-net'em II., king of Egypt, B.C. 1040. The right hand is laid upon the breast, and the left arm hangs by the side. The inscription reads:—

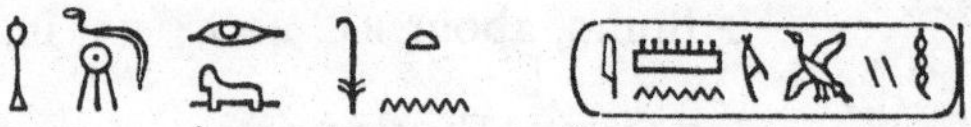 [1]

ḥet' Ȧusȧr suten Ȧmen-meri Pi-net'em

Shine upon Osiris, King, Pi-net'em, beloved of Ȧmen.

Thebes. Height, 4¾ in.

20. Blue glazed faïence *ushabti* figure of Pi-net'em II., king of Egypt, B.C. 1040. The inscription reads:—   *se-ḥet' Ȧusȧr χā-χeper-Rā Ȧmen-setep-[en] maātχeru.* Thebes. Height, 4¼ in.

21. Blue glazed faïence *ushabti* figure of Maāt-ka-Rā, a divine queen, about B.C. 1040. The inscription reads:— 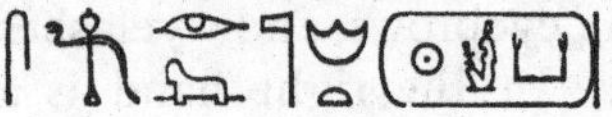 *se-ḥet' Ȧusȧr neter ḥemt Maāt-ka-Rā.* Thebes. Height, 4½ in.

22. Blue glazed faïence *ushabti* figure of Men-χeper-Rā (Pinet'em III.), king of Egypt, B.C. 1040. The inscription reads:—  (?) *se-ḥet' Ȧusȧr suten Men-χeper-Rā er ȧri kat.*

Thebes. Height, 5½ in.

23. Blue glazed faïence *ushabti* figure of the royal daughter and royal mother Ḥent-taiu 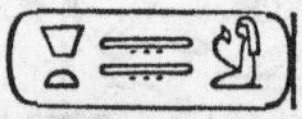, about B.C. 1040, inscribed with a version of the 6th chapter of the Book of the Dead. Thebes. Height, 6 in.

[1] For the history of the priest-kings, Pinet'em II., Pinet'em III., and the royal ladies Maāt-ka-Rā, Ḥent-taui, Nesi-chensu, Ȧuset-em-χebit, etc., see Maspero, *Les Momies Royales de Déir el-Bahari*, Paris, 1889.

24. Blue glazed faïence *ushabti* figure of , Nesi-chensu, a lady of the college of Àmen-Rā at Thebes, inscribed with part of the 6th chapter of the Book of the Dead. Height, $6\frac{3}{4}$ in.

25. Blue glazed faïence *ushabti* figure of 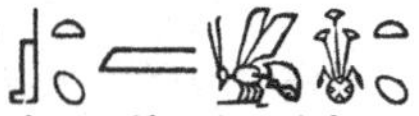 *Àuset em-χebit*, a queen, about B.C. 1040, inscribed with a version of the 6th chapter of the Book of the Dead.
Thebes. Height, $5\frac{5}{8}$ in.

26. Blue glazed faïence *ushabti* figure of  , *Nesi-ta-neb-àšer*, a princess, about B.C. 1040, inscribed with a version of the 6th chapter of the Book of the Dead. Thebes. Height, $5\frac{7}{8}$ in.

27-30. Four blue glazed faïence *ushabtiu* figures, inscribed:

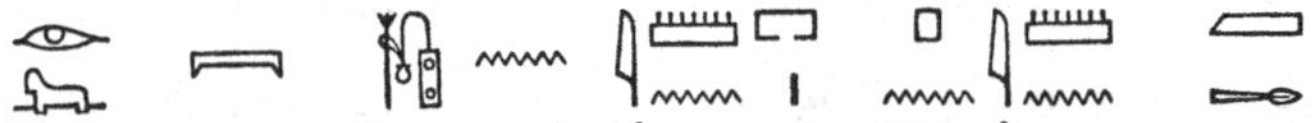

Àusàr ḥer ān en Àmen-pa Pen-Àmen maātχeru
"*Osiris, president of scribes of the Àmen temple, Pen-Àmen, triumphant*"!

The inscription on No. 28 reads:—   *seḥet' Àusàr āb Pen-Àmen.*
Thebes. Height, $3\frac{7}{8}$ in.

31. Upper part of a green glazed faïence *ushabti* figure made for a "divine father" of Àmen, called  Menθ-em-ḥāt, inscribed with a text different from that usually written on these figures. The fragments of the lines which remain are as follows:—

4.
5.

Thebes (?). Height, 7½ in.

32. Green glazed faïence *ushabtiu* figures made for a scribe called *Asher*, and inscribed with a version of the 6th chapter of the Book of the Dead. Height, 7¼ in.

33. Parts of green glazed faïence *ushabtiu* figures made for Uaḥ-àb-Rā, , a prophet (*neter ḥen*) of Bast (), and superintendent of . . . . , inscribed with a version of the 6th chapter of the Book of the Dead.

Heights, 6½ in. and 4¾ in.

34. Green glazed faïence *ushabti* figure made for

Åusår erpā ḥā Rā . . . . . Ḥeru mes en Ut'at-Śu maātχeru
"*Osiris, prince, duke, Rā . . . . . Ḥeru, born of Utchat-Shu, triumphant*"!

Height, 6 in.

35. Green glazed faïence *ushabti* figure with illegible inscription. Height, 5½ in.

36. Bluish-green glazed faïence *ushabti* figure made for *Sem-Åuset*, daughter of *Renp-nefer*.

Height, 4⅞ in.

37. Green glazed faïence *ushabti* figure made for "Psemθek (Psammetichus)-Seteb, child of Åru-ru" (?) (?)

Height, 5 in.

38. Upper part of green glazed faïence *ushabti* figure made for *Ta-Reṭet*, daughter of *Ta-Åmen* . . . .

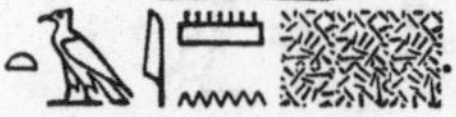

Height, 4 in.

39. Green glazed faïence *ushabti* figure made for 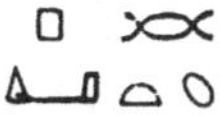 Pe-ṭā-Nit, inscribed with the 6th chapter of the Book of the Dead. Height, 4¼ in.

40. Green glazed faïence *ushabti* figure made for . . . . son of *Sta-u'tat*, triumphant  . . . . *mes Sta-ut'at maātχeru.* Height, 4⅛ in.

41. Green glazed faïence *ushabti* figure. Part of the inscription is effaced, and the other part is badly written and illegible. Height, 4⅛ in.

42. Green glazed faïence *ushabti* figure made for a woman whose name is illegible. Presented by the Rev. C. Beult. Height, 3¾ in.

43. Fragment of green glazed faïence *ushabti* figure.

44. Green glazed faïence *ushabti* figure uninscribed. Height, 2⅝ in.

45. Green glazed faïence *ushabti* figure with illegible name. Height, 4½ in.

46. Painted red terra-cotta *ushabti* figure made for "the lady of the house," Ḥent-met (?) 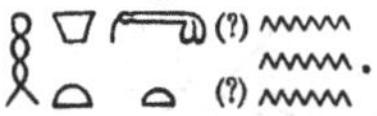. Height, 6¼ in.

47. Painted red terra-cotta *ushabti* figure made for a man whose name is illegible. Height, 5⅝ in.

48. Twelve uninscribed, rudely made terra-cotta and faïence *ushabtiu* figures.

49. Black, red, and yellow painted wooden *ushabti* figure made for Un-nefer, a priest of Chensu,  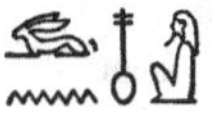 *āb en Chensu Un-nefer.* Height, 7¼ in.

50. Painted wood *ushabti* figure made for , Pai-net'em. Height, 7¾ in.

51. Painted wood *ushabti* figure inscribed  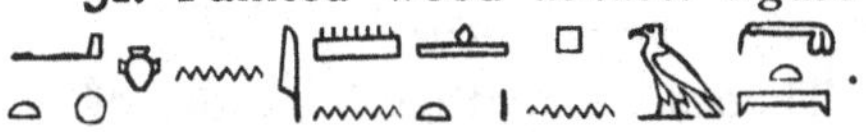. Height, 7½ in.

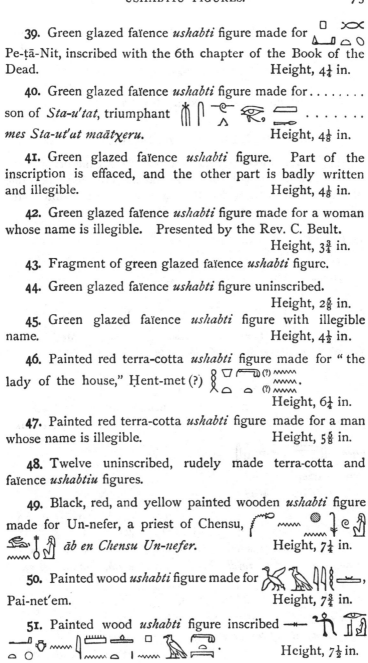

52. Painted wood *ushabti* figure, the characters on which appear to be modern. Height, 8½ in.

53. Painted wood *ushabti* figure uninscribed.
Height, 4¾ in.

54. Four uninscribed wooden *ushabtiu* figures.

MODELS OF OFFERINGS.

55. Red terra-cotta conical model of a cake or offering, inscribed, in relief, with the name and titles of Meri; portions of the colour with which the larger end was painted still adhere to the characters. The text reads:—

1. 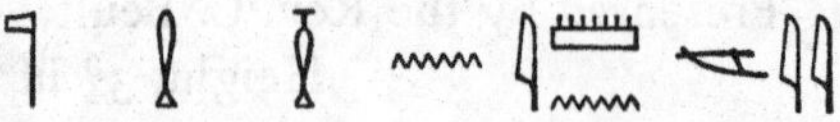

neter ḥen ḥes en Ȧmen Meri
Prophet singer of Ȧmen, Meri.

2. 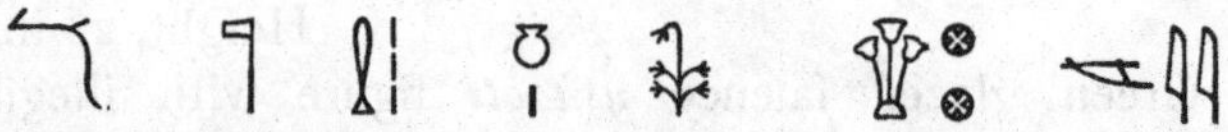

mer neter ḥen nu resu meḥt Meri
President of the prophets of the south and north, Meri.

3. 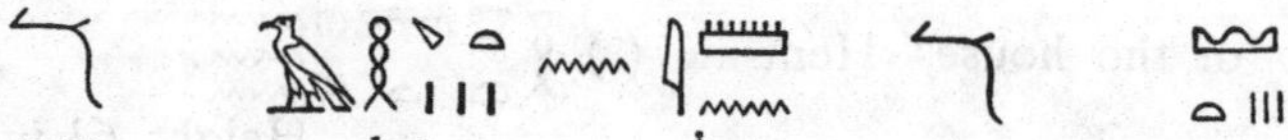

mer aḥet en Ȧmen mer set
Superintendent of the farms of Ȧmen, superintendent of the estates

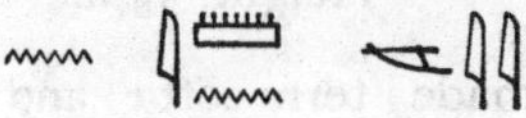

en Ȧmen Meri
of Ȧmen, Meri.

4. 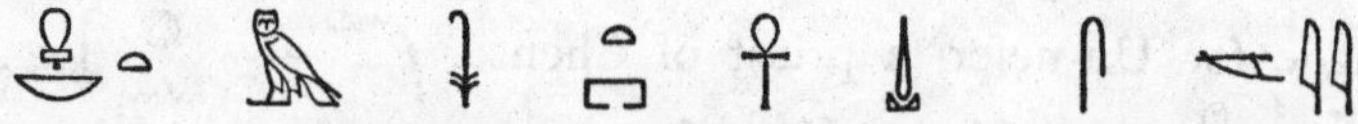

net em suten pa ānχ ut'a senb Meri
Chancellor in the royal house, life, strength, health, Meri.

5. 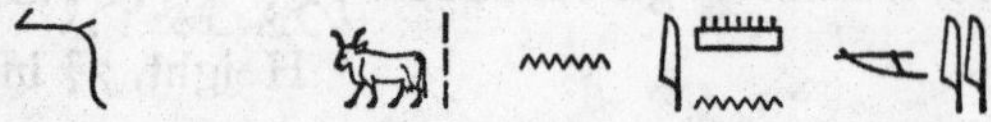

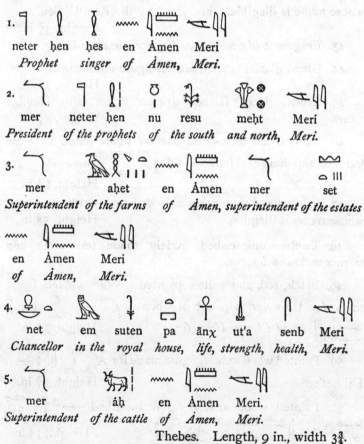

mer āḥ en Ȧmen Meri.
Superintendent of the cattle of Ȧmen, Meri.

Thebes. Length, 9 in., width 3¾.

56. Red terra-cotta conical model of a cake with three lines of inscription, in relief, which read :—

1. 

åmχi — χer
The watchful adorer — *before*

2. 

Åusår — suten — se — en — Keś
Osiris, — *the royal* — *son* — *of* — *Kush (Ethiopia),*

3. 

Meri - mes
Meri - mes.[1] XVIIIth dynasty. Thebes. Length, 6¾ in.

57. Red terra-cotta conical model of a cake inscribed, in relief, with figure of the deceased adoring the disk of the sun in the solar bark, and three lines of illegible hieroglyphics.

Thebes. Length, 6⅝ in.

SEPULCHRAL STELÆ.

58. Fragment of a limestone tablet of Ānch-meri (?), with figures of Anubis, Nephthys (?) and Thoth, in low relief, seated by the side of an altar, on which are laid three lotus flowers. Thoth is called "lord of  Cher-āba." The inscriptions over the altar, and Ānubis and Nephthys, are mutilated. Beneath this scene is a line of inscription which reads :—

Åusår āb en Men-χeper-Rā, em māt Ānχ-meri åri en
Osiris, priest of Men-χeper-Rā (Thothmes III.), ... Ānch-meri, son of . . . .

XVIIIth dynasty, B.C. 1600. 9½ in. × 7 in.

59. Limestone fragment inscribed with 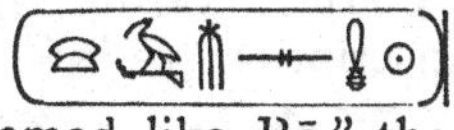 *χā må Rā Teḥuti-mes,* "Thothmes, diademed like Rā," the prenomen of Thothmes I., king of Egypt, about B.C. 1633.

[1] The cover of the coffin of this dignitary is in the British Museum (Egyptian Gallery, No. 1001). For an account of him see Brugsch, *Egypt under the Pharaohs,* Vol. I., p. 472, and Wiedemann, *Aegyptische Geschichte,* pp. 380, 394.

This fragment appears to have been cut out from one of the tombs at Thebes. XVIIIth dynasty. 21½ in. × 10 in.

60. Fragment of fine limestone from the wall of a temple or tomb, on which, in low relief, is a figure of the hawk of Horus, wearing the crowns of Upper and Lower Egypt, standing over the signs *ka neχt*, "mighty bull," which formed part of the "banner" name of the kings of the XVIIIth (?) dynasty.

Thebes or Abydos, XVIIIth(?) dynasty. 14 in. × 6½ in.

61. Fragment of fine limestone stele, inscribed with the figure of a king making an offering to a god; behind him stands the son "of his body," *en χat-f*, with libation vase. The cartouche which contained the name of the king is unfortunately mutilated. 18 in. × 12 in.

62. Rounded limestone tablet of Åmen-em-ḥeb, inscribed with the following scenes :—

1. Winged disk with uræi. Boat of Åmen-Rā, in which is a sepulchral chest, ornamented with buckles and *teṭs*, containing the mummy of the deceased lying on a bier; in the front of the boat, on a standard, is a bearded lion, having horns and plumes on his head. The ends of the boat terminate in rams' heads, each of which wears a disk, crown, plumes and uræi. The inscription reads :— 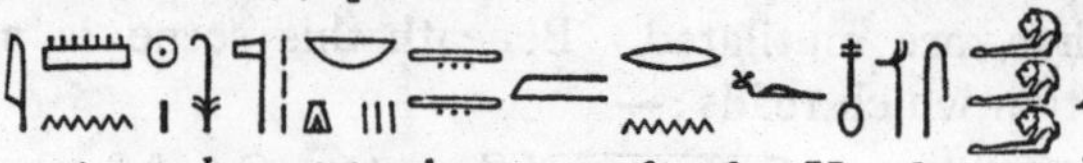 *Åmen-Rā suten neter neb nest taui em ren-f nefer Usr-ḥāu*, "Åmen-Rā, king of the gods, lord of the thrones of the two lands, in his beautiful name Usr-ḥāu."

2. Boat of Mut, wife of Åmen-Rā, in which is a shrine as in scene 1. Each end of the boat terminates in a head of Mut, wearing crowns of Upper and Lower Egypt. The inscription reads:—

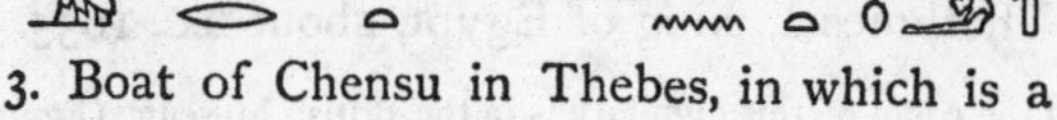 ......

3. Boat of Chensu in Thebes, in which is a shrine as in scenes 1 and 2. Each end of the boat terminates in a hawk's head, wearing disk and uræus. The inscription

reads :— 
χensu em Uast em ren-f θeḥen-ḥāt.

4. Heap of offerings, before which kneels the deceased 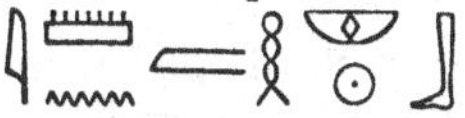 Åmen-em-ḥeb, with both hands raised in adoration ; behind him kneels 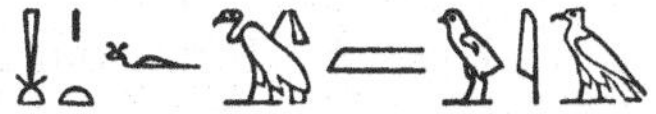 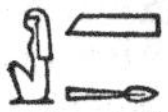 *sent-f Mut em-uåa maātχeru,* "His sister, Mut-em-uåa, triumphant." XXIInd dynasty. 22 in. × 16 in.

63. Limestone stele, rough hewn at sides and back, inscribed with the figure of a woman called Sent. Holding a lotus in her left hand, she stands before a table, upon which are laid a haunch of meat, , fruits, cakes , , and flowers. Above the table is a line of inscription, which reads :—

per χeru	χa	åḥ	apṭ	en	åmχet
Sepulchral meals,	*thousands of*	*oxen*	*and ducks*	*for*	*the watchful adorer*

Sent	mest	Ḥāpi	
Sent	*daughter of*	*Ḥāpi.*	9 in. × $8\frac{1}{2}$ in.

64. Limestone pyramidion, on the four sides of which are inscribed :—1. The deceased Åmsu-em-ḥeb kneeling, both hands raised in adoration. The inscription reads :  , *Ausår Åmsu-em-ḥeb ṭuau Rā Ḥeru-χuti em uben-f,* "Osiris, Åmsu-em-ḥeb. Adoration to Rā Harmachis when he shines." 2. Deceased kneeling as before, repetition of his name and *ṭuau Rā,* "Adoration to Rā." 3. Scene as on side No. 2. 4. Heaven, and the sun's disk on the horizon , and the name of the deceased , on each side of which is 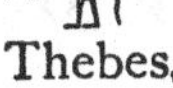.

Thebes, XXVIth dynasty. Length of side, 20in. ; base, 13 in.
(Presented by the Dean of Ely, 1827.)

65. Rectangular soft stone stele, made and inscribed for Rāi; the inscriptions on the top right hand corner are mutilated. On the upper half is a figure of Osiris, seated, holding and in his hands; on the back of his throne is the hawk of Horus, and behind stands "Isis, great lady, mistress of Amenta," wearing plumes. Before Osiris is a table of offerings, and by its side stands the deceased making an offering of lotus flowers and incense to the god. The inscription above reads, "May Osiris, at the head of Amenta, prince of the underworld, lord of Ṭeṭṭeṭ, within Abydos, lord of every god, give a royal oblation."[1] The mutilated inscription above the deceased Rāi states that he was "superintendent of the storehouse," and "triumphant before the lord of Amenta."

On the lower half of the stele is represented a table of offerings, to the left of which sit , *Ȧusȧr ḥer . . . . en neb pet Rāi*, "Osiris Rāi, chief of the storehouse of the lord of heaven," and *nebt pa Taθȧ*, "the lady of the house Taθȧ." The deceased Rāi and Pepi hold the *χerp* sceptre in their hands. To the right of the table sit *Ȧusȧr Pepi maāt-χeru neb ȧmχi*, "Osiris Pepi, triumphant, lord of watchful adoration," and *qemā en neb nehet resu Tai maātχeru*, "Tai, the lady of the college of the lord of southern sycamore, triumphant"!

XXVIth dynasty. 3 ft. 6 in. × 2 ft. 2 in.

66. Upper part of a rounded sandstone stele on which are inscribed:—1. Winged disk, with uræi, having hanging

1 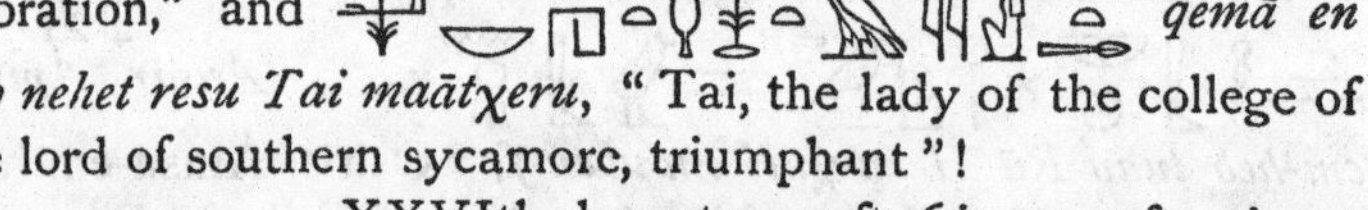

from the neck of each; under each wing is inscribed *Beḥutet neter āa*, "Behutet, great god." 2. The deceased, a woman, standing by the side of a table, and a libation vase on stand, adoring Rā-Harmachis, who wears and holds and in his hands. The inscription reads:— , *Ḥeru-χuti neter āa neb pet neteru*, "Harmachis, great god, lord of heaven and of the gods." 3. The deceased adoring the god Tmu, who wears the crowns of the north and south, and holds and in his hands. The inscription reads:— , *Tmu neb taui Ȧnnu*, "Atmu, lord of the two lands and Heliopolis." These scenes are divided from the inscription which occupied the lower part of the tablet by a line of *χakeru* ornaments, .

This tablet was made during the period immediately preceding the Ptolemies. 14½ in. × 11¼ in.

67. Upper part of a rounded, roughly made limestone stele on which are inscribed *śen*, , and two lines of inscription which entreat the god Osiris to give sepulchral meals to the deceased, . Under this, the deceased stands by the side of a table of offerings, in the presence of Osiris seated; on the table are cakes, fruits, and flowers. In the scene beneath are "the father of his mother," and "the mother of his mother, the lady of the house," each by the side of a table of offerings . The inscriptions read:—

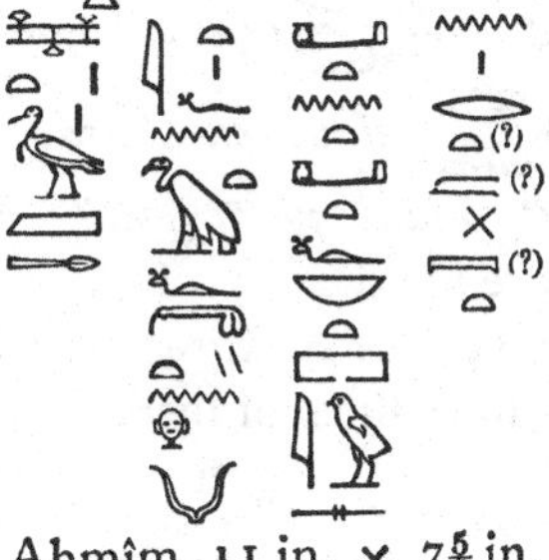

Aḥmîm, 11 in. × 7⅝ in.

68. Limestone stele of Er-årit-ru (?) inscribed with winged disk and pendent uræi, and a scene in which the deceased lady is represented standing with her son (?) by the side of a table of offerings, with both hands raised in adoration to Rā, hawk-headed, and wearing . The inscription reads:—

Rā Ḥeru-χuti neb pet Seb erpā neteru
Rā Harmachis, lord of heaven, Seb, prince of the gods,

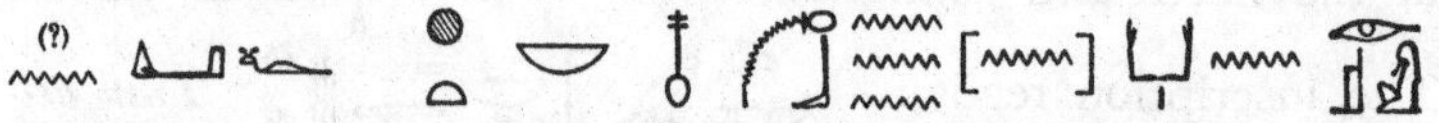

. . . . ṭā - f χet neb nefer āb en ka en Åusår
may give he things all good, pure to the ka of Osiris,

Er - årit - ru (?) maātχeru se en Ḥeru, maātχeru.
Er - årit - ru (?), triumphant, son of Ḥeru, triumphant!

On the side is *Rā neter āa neb pet,* "Rā, great god, lord of heaven."

Aḥmîm. Ptolemaic period. 11½ in. × 7 in.

69. Rounded limestone stele, on the upper part of which are inscribed Isis , Osiris, lord of eternity , and the deceased, who says, "

, *åaui en Åusår sen-ta ren-f en ka en . . . . . em en årit niåai maātχeru,*" "Adores Osiris, whose name be adored! the *ka* of . . . ., triumphant"! Beneath are the figures of three women and one man, and above them are nine lines of inscription which read:—

Mut-f θes en Ȧusȧr Ȧuset χāθ maātχeru neb pa-f Tabaḥ maātχeru set-f Tahamu maātχeru se-f Pa-unen se-f Unnefer maātχeru se-f Pa-Bes. 1. His mother was Auset-chāā-th, a singer of Osiris, triumphant! Tabaḥ was the lady of his house, triumphant! Tahamu was his daughter, triumphant! Pa-unen was his son, Un-nefer was his son, triumphant! Pa-Bes was his son, triumphant!

Aḥmîm, Ptolemaic period. 16 in. × 8½ in.

70. Rounded limestone stele of Pekkem, on the upper part of which is a scene in which the deceased is standing by the side of a table of offerings adoring Osiris, Isis, and Nephthys. Above is the winged disk with pendent uræi, and below are four lines of partly erased inscription which read :—

1. 

2. 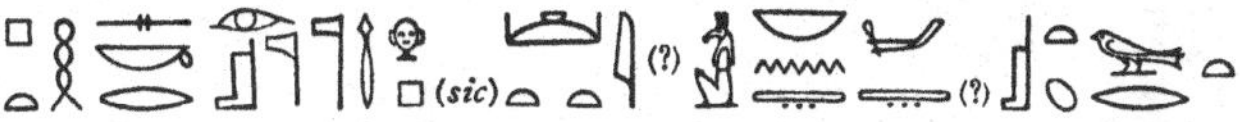

3. 

4. 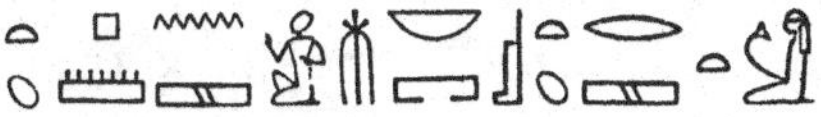

1. *Suten ḥetep ṭa Ȧusȧr χent Ȧmenta neter āa neb Ȧbṭu Seker Ȧusȧr ḥer ȧb Ȧpu*

2. *Ptaḥ-Seker-Ȧusȧr neter āa ḥer ȧatet Ȧnpu neb en ta-serta Ȧuset urt*

3. *neter mut ṭā-s perχeru ḥeq ȧḥ ȧpt ȧχet neb nefer ab en ka en p kekem*

4. *set P-menś mes neb pa Ȧuset-reśt.*

"May Osiris, at the head of the underworld, the great god, lord of Abydos, and Seker-Osiris within Apu (Panopolis), and Ptah-Seker-Osiris, great god, resident of the tomb, and Anubis, lord of the Holy Land, and Isis, great lady, divine mother, give sepulchral meals of beer, beef, ducks, and all good and beautiful things to the genius of P'-kekem, daughter of P-mensh, born of the lady of the house, Åuset-reshet."

Ahmîm, Ptolemaic period, 16 in. × 12 in.

71. Upper part of a stone stele. Deceased, seated, holding a flower , to his nose, and his son, standing by the side of a table of offerings, pouring out a libation  before him. Above are the two *ut'ats*  and  *śen.*

From Karnak. 6½ in. × 4¾ in.

72. Sandstone fragment, from one of the Ptolemaic temples of Egypt, with figures in relief of the three spirits of the dawn. 10 in. × 6 in.

73 Sandstone fragment, from one of the Ptolemaic temples of Egypt, with parts of two lines of inscription in relief. 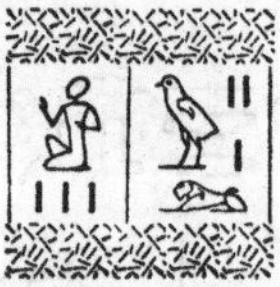 10¼ in. × 6 in.

74. Sandstone fragment, from one of the Græco-Roman temples of Egypt, with a serpent wearing crown and plumes in relief, and an inscription which reads:—

 *se-s mer-s meru.* 20½ in. × 15 in.

75. Rounded sandstone stele, the front of which has been painted a bright red colour. On it are inscribed: 1. The goddess Isis, wearing disk and horns, and holding in her hand the sceptre  *uat';* before her is a table loaded with offerings. Above is inscribed [Isis] lady of . . . . 2. The deceased standing by the side of a table of offerings, making an offering. Behind him stand his wife and son holding  *nif* in the right hand, and a palm branch in the left. The names of all three are much effaced, but that of the man for whom the tablet was made appears to have been , Ȧpepi. The right hand bottom corner of the tablet is broken away. 12 in. × 9in.

76. Limestone tablet of Thatha, in the form of a door, the upper part of which is in the form of a cornice of palm leaves, painted in green and red. The first two lines of inscription read:—

suten ḥetep ṭā Ȧusȧr neter āa neb Ȧbṭu ṭā - f

"*May give royal oblation Osiris, god great, lord of Abydos, may give he*

perχeru ȧḥ ȧpt sennu neter senθra merḥet

sepulchral meals of oxen, ducks, cakes, incense, wax,

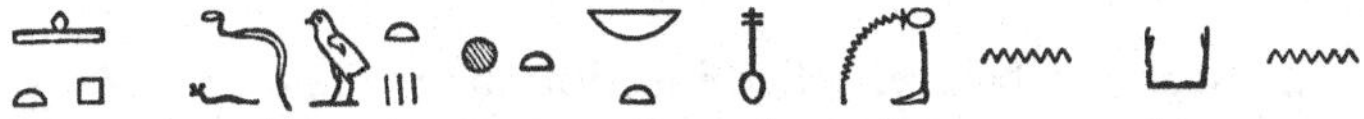

ḥetep t'efaut χet nebt nefer āb en ka en

offerings of Tchefau food, things all good, pure, to the genius of the

net suten . . . . ṡes Θȧθȧ maātχeru

chancellor . . . . royal . . . . Thatha, triumphant"!

Beneath are the following scenes:—1. Table of offerings , on the left of which is seated the deceased; on the right is a young man standing with one arm raised, and by his side an older man seated at a table of offerings. Over the standing figure is inscribed 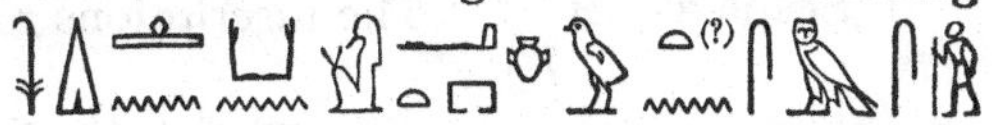  *suten ḥetep ṭā en ka en ȧri āt ȧbu . . . . sems mes en Ki*, "Give a royal oblation to the genius of the guardian of the hall, ... the controller, born of Ki"; and over the seated

figure behind him 
 (?)  (?) *suten ṭā ḥetep en ka en àri āt àbu χent-χaθi-ḥetep maāχeru mes en Tenkth* (?).

2. Two men seated at table of offerings, above which is inscribed :—

3. Scene as before. The inscriptions read :—

4. Scene as before. The inscriptions read :—

5. Scene as before. The inscriptions read :—

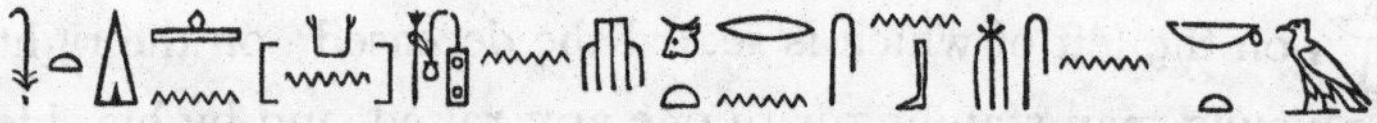

6. Scene as before. The inscriptions read :—

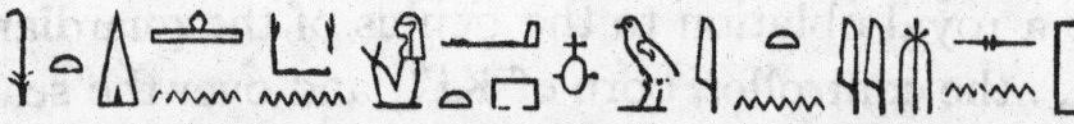

7. Table of offerings. On the left is 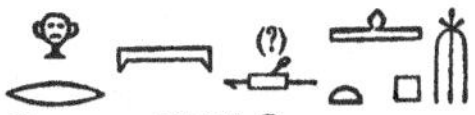  and on the right 

2 ft. × 14½ in.

Presented by the late Very Rev. G. Peacock, Dean of Ely, 1840.

Sepulchral Statues of Karemā and Abui.

77. Seated figure of the scribe Karemā, surnamed *Ḳer-Uast*, "the landlord of Thebes," holding a palette and reeds in his right hand, and a whip in his left; both hands are crossed over the breast. By his side is seated "his sister Ȧbui, the lady of the house,"  *sent-f nebt pa Ȧbui.* Between the two figures is inscribed  .

On the two sides of the seat are upright figures of his four sons in relief, each holding a lotus flower in one of his hands. The inscriptions read :—

 *se-f Neb-neteru,* "his son Neb-neteru."

 *se-f Se-mut,* "his son Se-mut."

 *se-f Qen-Ȧmen,* "his son Qen-Ȧmen."

 *se-f Mā-ḥu,* "his son Māḥu."

In front of the seat are the unnamed figure of a boy painted in red, and that of a woman holding a lotus flower; she is called 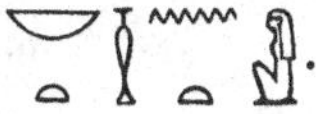.

On the back of this group is inscribed :—

1. 

Suten ṭā ḥetep Ȧusȧr χent Ȧmenti

May give a royal oblation, Osiris, at the head of the underworld

Ȧnpu

and Anubis

2. 

åm ut neb Ta-ser ṭā-sen

in the sarcophagus, lord of the Holy Land, may give they

pert χerut ta ḥeq åḥ apt menχet neter sentrå merḥet

sepulchral meals, cakes, beer, oxen, ducks, bandages, incense, wax,

3. 

χet neb nefert ābt χet neb net'emet bener ṭāṭā

things all beautiful, pure, things all sweet and pleasant, of the gifts of

pet qem

heaven, of the products of

4. 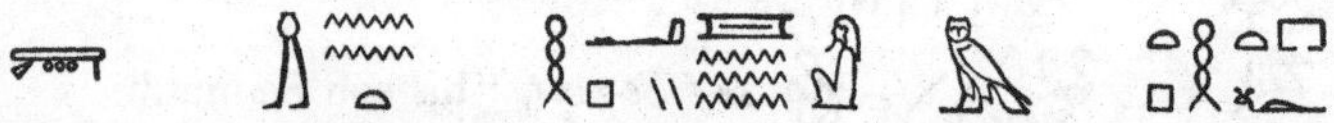

ta ånnet Ḥāpi em tepḥet - f

earth, of the bringing of Ḥāpi out of storehouse his,

5. 

en ka en ān Ka - re - mā maātχeru

to the ka of the scribe Karema, triumphant!

6. 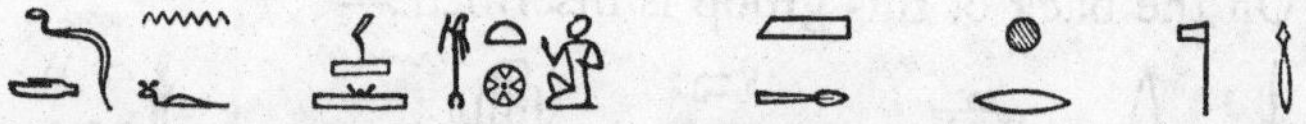

t'eṭ - nef ḳer - Uast maātχeru χer neter āa

called is he, "landlord of Thebes," triumphant before the god great.

Above the inscription are  and ; the hieroglyphics are inlaid in blue.

Thebes. XIXth dynasty. Height, 15¾ in.

SCARABS FROM MUMMIES AND RINGS, ETC.

78. Green stone scarab, with setting of gold, inscribed on the base with the 30th chapter (B) of the Book of the Dead. The text reads :—

TRANSLITERATION.

1. T'eṭ-f àb-à en mut-à sep sen
2. ḥāti-à χeperu-à em āḥā er-à
3. [em] meteru em se-χesefu er-à em
4. t'at'anut em àritu āk er-à em
5. baḥ àri māχait entek ka-à àmi χat-à
6. χnemu se-ut'a āt-à per-k er bu
7. nefer ḥen en n àm em seχen ren-n en
8. śenit àriu ret em āḥāu
9. nefer en n nefer setem āu àb ut'ā t'eṭtu em qem-
10. ṭu ḳer er-à erma neter māk
11. tent-k un-*θ*à

TRANSLATION.

1. *Says he, "O heart mine of my mother! O heart mine of my mother!*
2. *O heart mine of my evolutions! Let there be no obstruction to me*
3. *in evidence, nor stoppage to me by*
4. *the divine chiefs; mayest thou not fall away from me*
5. *before the guardian of the Scale. Thou art my genius in my body.*
6. *The god Chnemu makes strong my limbs. Come thou to the place of*
7. *happiness to which we go. May not make to stink our name*
8. *the Shenit, who make men strong.*
9. *Pleasant to us, pleasant is the joyful hearing at the weighing of words. May*
10. *not be made against me false accusation in the presence of the great god!*
11. *Verily, exceedingly mighty art thou when thou risest"!*

Thebes. $2\frac{3}{8}$ in. long.

79. White glazed steatite oval inscribed *Cheperá-men*, "Chepera the stablisher." Length, $\frac{1}{2}$ in.

80. Yellowish bronze glazed steatite scarab inscribed with a beetle, the emblem of the god *Cheperá*.

Length, $\frac{5}{8}$ in.

81. Red hard-stone scarab inscribed *Rā ṭeṭ*, "Rā, the stable one." Length, $\frac{9}{16}$ in.

82. Brown glazed steatite scarab inscribed *Rā-χeper*, "Rā the creator." Length, $\frac{5}{8}$ in.

83. Yellow paste scarab inscribed *Rā-neb*, "Rā the lord." Naucratis. Length, $\frac{1}{2}$ in.

84. Light blue glazed steatite scarab inscribed with kneeling king, and *Rā ānχ nefer ḥes*, "Rā the bestower of a happy life." Length, $\frac{3}{4}$ in.

85. Brownish-green glazed scarab inscribed *Rā men taiu neferu*, "Rā establishing the two lands [by his] beauties."

Length, $\frac{3}{4}$ in.

86. Steatite scarab inscribed *Rā-neferu-uaḥ*, "Rā the bestower of beauties." Around this name, or motto, are a double set of *ānχ ṭeṭ ānχ*, "life, stability, life."

Length, $1\frac{5}{16}$ in.

87. Yellow glazed steatite scarab inscribed "Åmen-Rā." Length, $\frac{5}{8}$ in.

88. Green glazed faïence oblong plaque. Obverse, figure of god holding *ānχ* in his right hand; reverse, the name *Åmen-Rā*, "Amen-Rā." Length, $\frac{3}{4}$ in.

89. White glazed steatite scarab inscribed *Åmen-Rā.* Length, $\frac{3}{4}$ in.

90. Green glazed faïence human-headed scarab inscribed *Åmen-Rā.* Length, $1\frac{1}{8}$ in.

91. Brownish-gray glazed steatite scarab inscribed [(?)] *Åmen-Rā* (?). Length, $\frac{3}{4}$ in.

92. Lapis-lazuli oval. Obverse *Åmen-Rā.* Reverse .

Length, $\frac{11}{16}$ in.

93. Gray glazed steatite scarab inscribed *Åmen-Rā neter nefer neb taiu*, "Åmen-Rā, beautiful god, lord of two worlds." Length, $\frac{3}{4}$ in.

94. Green glazed faïence scarab inscribed *Åmen-Rā neb maāt*, Åmen-Rā, the lord of law." Length, $\frac{5}{8}$ in.

95. Brown glazed steatite scarab inscribed *χut neb Ḥeru.*

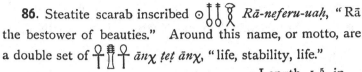

Length, $\frac{1}{2}$ in.

96. Gray glazed steatite scarab inscribed with *Åmsu*, and curved line ornament. Length, $\frac{7}{16}$ in.

97. Greenish-yellow glazed steatite scarab, inscribed with the names of the gods Ptaḥ and Maāt. Length, $\frac{9}{16}$ in.

98. Light blue glazed faïence scarab, inscribed with Neith and two uræi. Naucratis. Length, $\frac{7}{8}$ in.

99. Brown glazed steatite scarab inscribed *Chensu em sa*, "Chensu is protector."

Length, $\frac{1}{2}$ in.

100. Whitish glazed steatite scarab inscribed with two uræi, double *ānχ*, emblem of the god Cheperȧ, and the name *Nefer ḥetep.* Length, $\frac{5}{16}$ in.

101. Yellow composition scarab inscribed with figure of the god Bes. Naucratis. Length $1\frac{1}{8}$ in.

102. Yellow glazed steatite scarab inscribed with a figure of the god Bes and two uræi. Length, $\frac{7}{8}$ in.

103. Dark brown glazed steatite scarab inscribed with figure of the god Bes, and a lion-headed god, wearing the feather on his head. Length, $1\frac{1}{8}$ in.

Scarabs inscribed with Names of Kings.

104. Black stone cylinder, pierced, inscribed with the name of Saḥu-Rā, the second king of the Vth dynasty, about B.C. 3533.

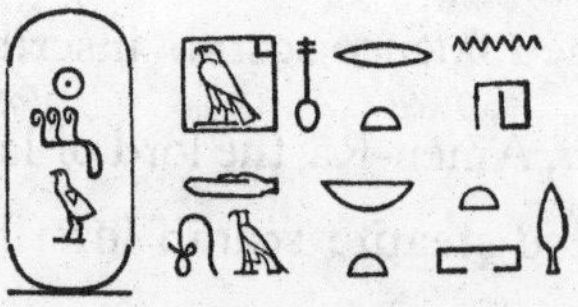

Saḥu-Rā. Ḥetḥert ṭua nefert nebt Nehet

"*Saḥu-Rā. . . . . . Hathor, beautiful, lady of the Sycamore.*"

Length, $\frac{5}{8}$ in.

105. Gray glazed steatite scarab inscribed with cartouche containing *Rā-neb-χeru*, the prenomen of Menthu-ḥetep V., king of Egypt, about B.C. 2500. Length, $\frac{1}{2}$ in.

106. Light green glazed Egyptian faïence scarab inscribed *ka-χeper-Rā*, on each side of which are . On the back of the scarab is a head of Hathor (?) wearing plumes and head-dress. The characters on the cartouche are probably meant to recall those forming the prenomen of Usertsen I., *Rā-χeper-ka*, the second king of the XIIth dynasty, B.C. 2433. Length, $1\frac{1}{2}$ in.

107. White glazed steatite scarab inscribed *i.e.*, *χeper-ka-Rā*, prenomen of Usertsen I. (?). Length, $\frac{9}{16}$ in.

108. Steatite cylinder inscribed *Nub-kau-Rā*, the prenomen of Åmenemḥāt II., third king of the XIIth dynasty, B.C. 2400. Length, $\frac{3}{4}$ in.

109. Gray-green glazed steatite scarab inscribed with figure of an animal holding a sceptre, child with his finger in his mouth, and cartouche containing the prenomen of Ka-mes, *Uat'-χeper-Rā*, king of Egypt about B.C. 1700. Length, $\frac{11}{16}$ in.

110. Green glazed steatite scarab inscribed *Men-χeper-Rā ḥetep ḥer maāt*, "Men-χeper-Rā resting upon Law." The cartouche contains the prenomen of Thothmes III., king of Egypt, B.C. 1600. Length, $\frac{5}{8}$ in.

111. Cobalt-blue glazed steatite scarab inscribed *Suten Rā-χeper-men*, "king Rā-χeper-men" (Thothmes III. ?). Length, $\frac{1}{2}$ in.

112. Yellowish-gray steatite plaque. Obverse, title of Thothmes III., *ānχ Ḥeru ka*, "living Horus, bull [mighty]," and seated figures of Rā  and Horus. Reverse, double prenomen of Thothmes III. 1$\frac{3}{4}$ in. × 1$\frac{1}{4}$ in.

113. Gray glazed steatite scarab, inscribed with prenomen of Thothmes III., figure of the goddess Maāt , and 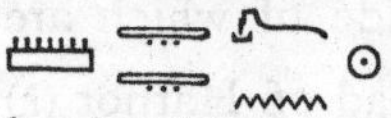 *men taiu setep en Rā*, "establisher of the two lands, chosen of Rā." Length, $\frac{3}{4}$ in.

114. Brown glazed hard-stone scarab, inscribed with the prenomen of Thothmes III.,  *Rā-men-χeper*. Above it are a lion , and uræus , and on each side is an uræus wearing a disk. The scarab is ram-headed, and on each wing is a winged uræus. The hieroglyphics are lighter in colour than the groundwork of the base. Length, 1$\frac{5}{16}$ in.

115. Yellow glazed steatite scarab, inscribed with:—1.  *χeper*,  *ḥeq*, and  *ārat*, *i.e.*, the emblems of creation, rule, and divinity; 2. cartouche containing prenomen of Thothmes III., , on each side of which is a vulture; and 3. beetle , on each side of which is an uræus . Length, 1$\frac{3}{4}$ in.

116. Gray glazed steatite scarab inscribed with cartouche containing the prenomen of Thothmes III., , and the title 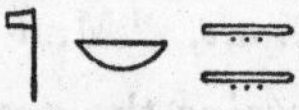 *neter neb taiu*, "god, lord of the two countries," and a bearded, man-headed sphinx , and an indistinct object. Length, $\frac{11}{16}$ in.

117. Yellow glazed steatite scarab inscribed with the prenomen of Thothmes III.,  *neter nefer neb taiu*, "beautiful god, lord of the two earths," and the name of the god  *Ȧmen-Rā*, "Ȧmen-Rā." Length, $\frac{5}{8}$ in.

118. Yellow glazed steatite scarab inscribed with the prenomen of Thothmes III., double *maāt*, and the name of the god *Åmen-Rā*, "Åmen-Rā." Length, $\frac{5}{8}$ in.

119. Brown glazed steatite scarab, inscribed with the figure of a king, crowned and holding, the emblem of rule, in his left hand, the prenomen of Thothmes III., *Rā-men-χeper*, and the name of the god *Åmen-Rā.* Length, $\frac{1}{2}$ in.

120. Green glazed steatite scarab inscribed *Rā-men-χeperȧ*, the prenomen of Thothmes III.

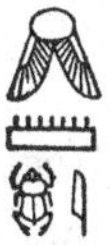

Length, $1\frac{1}{16}$ in.

121. Brown glazed steatite scarab inscribed with double prenomen of Thothmes III., and *χeper uā χeper*, "Cheperȧ, only one, creator."

Length, $\frac{11}{16}$ in.

122. Green glazed steatite scarab inscribed with the prenomen of Thothmes III. on each side of which are two uræi.

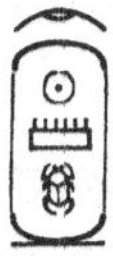

Length, $\frac{1}{2}$ in.

123. Yellow glazed steatite scarab, inscribed with double prenomen of Thothmes III., and *neter nefer neb taiu*, "Beautiful god, lord of the two lands." Length, $\frac{13}{16}$ in.

124. Brown glazed steatite scarab inscribed with prenomen of Thothmes III., and *ḥetep ḥer maāt*, "resting upon law." Length, $\frac{11}{16}$ in.

125. Yellowish-green glazed square steatite plaque. Obverse, a tree, on each side of which are two apes. Reverse, *Rā-men-χeper*, enclosed in a square border.

$1\frac{3}{8} \times 1$ in.

126. Light brown glazed steatite scarab inscribed with the prenomen of Thothmes III., *Rā-men-χeper*, scarab *χeper*, and double . Length, $\frac{3}{4}$ in.

127. Brown glazed steatite scarab inscribed with a winged disk, cartouche containing the prenomen of Thothmes III., , figure of the god Bes, and two prisoners.

Length, $1\frac{1}{4}$ in.

128. Dark gray glazed steatite scaraboid with two winged disks and the prenomen of Thothmes III. On the upper side are spiral ornaments. Length, 1 in.

129. Green glazed steatite scarab inscribed with winged disk, cartouche containing the prenomen of Thothmes III., (*sic*), and beetle , emblem of the god Cheperá, on each side of which are an uræus and *neb*.

Length, $1\frac{7}{8}$ in.

130. Gray glazed steatite scarab inscribed *Rā-men-χeper*, the prenomen of Thothmes III., enclosed in border of spiral ornament. Length, $\frac{5}{8}$ in.

131. Brown glazed steatite scarab inscribed with the prenomen of Thothmes III., *Rā-men-χeper*, a sphinx , and an indistinct sign. Length, $\frac{5}{8}$ in.

132. Brown glazed steatite scarab inscribed *Rā-men-χeper* and the emblem of Law, *maāt*. Length $\frac{5}{8}$ in.

133. Dark gray steatite cowroid inscribed with the prenomen of Thothmes III. and floral ornaments.

Length, $2\frac{1}{8}$ in.

134. Light yellow glazed scarab inscribed with the prenomen of Thothmes III., jackal (Anubis), and mouse (?).

Length $\frac{7}{8}$ in.

135. Green glazed steatite scarab inscribed with the prenomen of Thothmes III., and winged disks with uræi.

Length, $\frac{5}{8}$ in.

136. Greenish-gray steatite scarab inscribed with the prenomen of Thothmes III., on each side of which is an uræus , below is a winged beetle with asps. Length, $\frac{5}{8}$ in.

137. Yellow glazed steatite scarab inscribed with the prenomen of Thothmes III. and vulture. Length, $\frac{1}{2}$ in.

138. Gray glazed steatite scarab inscribed with a cartouche containing the prenomen of Thothmes III., 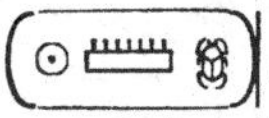, and  *ānχ Ḥeru tā* . . . . "the living Horus. . . . ." Length, $\frac{3}{4}$ in.

139. Blue glazed steatite plaque. Obverse, figure of the god Set and king; reverse, slightly rounded, inscribed *Rā-taiu* (?) *men-χeper.* Thothmes III (?). 

Length, $\frac{3}{4}$ in.

140. Green glazed steatite oval, obverse,  *maāt,* emblem of "law," and  *Āa-χeperu-Rā,* the prenomen of Amenophis II., king of Egypt, B.C. 1566. Reverse, figure of the god Ptaḥ  and the legend  *p ḥrȧ nefer,* "the beautiful face." Length, $\frac{9}{16}$ in.

141. Gray glazed steatite scarab inscribed  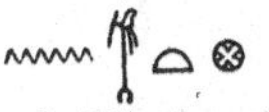 *Neb-Maāt-Rā mer en Uast,* "Neb-maāt-Rā beloved of Thebes." The cartouche contains the prenomen of Amenophis III., B.C. 1500. Length, $1\frac{5}{8}$ in.

142. Steatite scarab inscribed *Neb-maāt-Rā* 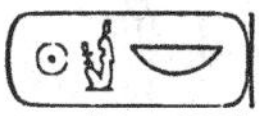. The cartouche contains the prenomen of Amenophis III., B.C. 1500. Length, $\frac{5}{8}$ in.

143. Green glazed steatite scarab inscribed with cartouche containing the prenomen of Amenophis III., 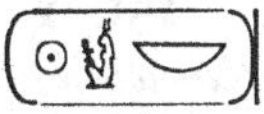 *Neb-maāt-Rā,* on each side of which is an uræus wearing a disk. Length, $\frac{5}{8}$ in.

144. Blue glazed steatite scarab inscribed with cartouche containing the prenomen of Amenophis III., *Neb-maāt-Rā*, and *neb śuti*, "lord of plumes."

Length, $\frac{5}{8}$ in.

145. Green glazed steatite scarab inscribed with cartouche containing the prenomen of Chut-en-âten or Amenophis IV., *Rā-neferu-χeper-uā-en-Rā*, king of Egypt, about B.C. 1500.

Length, $\frac{1}{2}$ in.

146. Yellow glazed steatite scarab (broken), on which is inscribed the figure of a king offering two vessels to a cynocephalus ape wearing disk and crescent; above is *Usr-maāt-Rā*, perhaps part of the prenomen (?) of Rameses II., king of Egypt, B.C. 1333.

Length, $\frac{3}{4}$ in.

147. Pink glazed steatite scarab inscribed *Rā-usr-Maāt setep en [Á]men-Rā*, perhaps the prenomen of Osorkon II., king of Egypt, B.C. 866.

Length, $\frac{9}{16}$ in.

148. Gray glazed scarab inscribed with *Rā-ḥet'-χeper*, perhaps a part of the prenomen of Θekeleth II., *Ḥet'-χeper-Rā setep-en-Rā*, the sixth king of the XXIInd dynasty, B.C. 833.

Length, $\frac{1}{2}$ in.

149. Brownish yellow glazed steatite scarab inscribed [1] *Rā-men-āa-nefer*, double , double uræus , and .

Length, $\frac{3}{4}$ in.

150. Dark gray steatite scarab inscribed *Nefer em χet maāt.*

Length, $\frac{11}{16}$ in.

151. Yellow glazed steatite scarab inscribed *Rā-neb-maāt.*

Length, $\frac{1}{2}$ in.

[1] We might read *uat'*.

SCARABS INSCRIBED WITH THE NAMES OF PRIVATE PERSONS.

152. Gray glazed steatite scarab inscribed on base with  *Rā-Sebek*(?)*neb.* Found at Ephesus.

Length, $\frac{7}{16}$ in.

153. Light green glazed scarab inscribed 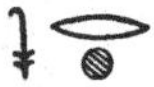 *suten reχ*, "royal kinsman." Length, $\frac{9}{16}$ in.

154. Light gray glazed steatite scarab inscribed

Length, $\frac{7}{8}$ in.

155. White glazed steatite scarab inscribed on base

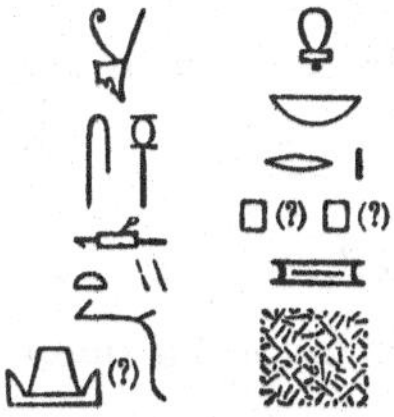

Length, $\frac{7}{8}$ in.

156. Light gray glazed steatite scarab inscribed

Length, $\frac{7}{16}$ in.

157. White glazed steatite scarab inscribed   *net mer pa ser*(?) *Ākȧ*, "Ākȧ, the chancellor, president of the temple. . . . ."

Length, $\frac{7}{8}$ in.

158. Brown glazed steatite scarab inscribed

Length, $\frac{11}{16}$ in.

159. Composition scarab inscribed

Length, $\frac{7}{8}$ in.

160. Yellow glazed steatite scarab inscribed

Length, $\frac{5}{8}$ in.

161. Yellow paste scarab inscribed 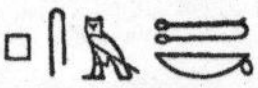 *Psemθek*, "Psammetichus." Naucratis. Length, $\frac{1}{2}$ in.

162. Yellow glazed steatite scarab inscribed 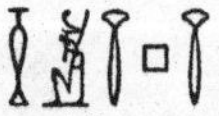 *ḥes Ȧmen* (?) *uat' p uat'*, "favoured one of Ȧmen. . . . . ."
Length, $\frac{9}{16}$ in.

163. Gray glazed steatite scarab inscribed 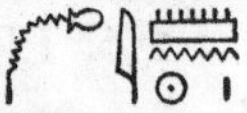 *āb Ȧmen-Rā*, "a priest of Ȧmen-Rā." Length, $\frac{1}{2}$ in.

164. Light blue glazed steatite scarab inscribed 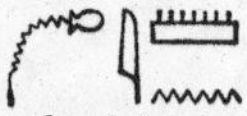  (*sic*) *āb Ȧmen-Rā*, "priest of Ȧmen-Rā." Length, $\frac{1}{2}$ in.

165. Steatite scarab inscribed  *ḥes Ȧmen*, "the favoured one of Ȧmen." Naucratis. Length, $\frac{7}{16}$ in.

166. Yellowish-green glazed paste scarab inscribed  *se Rā*, "child of Rā." Naucratis. Length, $\frac{7}{16}$ in.

167. Gray glazed steatite scarab inscribed *ḥes* . . . flower (?), and a figure of some animal. Length, $\frac{5}{8}$ in.

168. Light yellow glazed steatite scarab inscribed with cynocephalus ape of Thoth *Ḥeru ḥes*, "favoured one of Horus," and sphinx. Length, $\frac{9}{16}$ in.

169. Dark yellow steatite scarab inscribed with couchant animal wearing double plumes, winged uræus, and *ḥes maāt*, "favoured one of Maat." Length, $\frac{1}{2}$ in.

170. Yellow paste scarab inscribed on base *ḥes Āāḥ*, "the favoured one of the Moon-god."

Naucratis. Length, $\frac{7}{16}$ in.

171. Light green glazed steatite scarab inscribed *neter neb ḥes*, "favoured of the great god." Fine workmanship. Length, $\frac{9}{16}$ in.

172. Brown glazed steatite scarab inscribed with  and four wings (?).

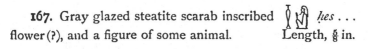

Length, $\frac{3}{4}$ in.

173. Yellow stone plaque or bead, square, and pierced, inscribed 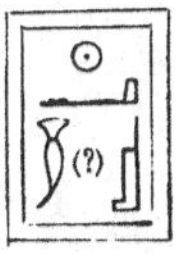 *Rā-bener* (?)-*Āuset*. Length, $\frac{9}{16}$ in.

SCARABS, ETC., INSCRIBED WITH DEVICES, EMBLEMS, MOTTOES, ETC.

174. Brown glazed flat steatite bead. Obverse , reverse . Length, $\frac{1}{2}$ in.

175. Green glazed steatite scarab inscribed on base 

Length, $\frac{5}{8}$ in.

176. Light blue glazed *faïence* oval inscribed 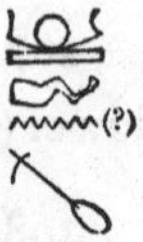
Length, $\frac{9}{16}$ in.

177. Light gray glazed scarab inscribed on base 
Length, $\frac{9}{16}$ in.

178. Dark brown glazed steatite scarab inscribed 
Length, $\frac{3}{4}$ in.

179. Light yellow glazed steatite scarab inscribed 
Length, $\frac{5}{8}$ in.

180. Brown glazed steatite scarab inscribed 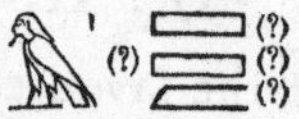
 *ba . . . . . ṭā ānχ.* Length, $\frac{5}{8}$ in.

181. Brown glazed steatite scarab inscribed 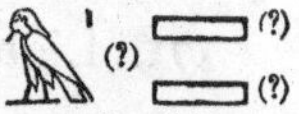
 *ba . . . . . . ṭā ānχ.* Length, $\frac{5}{8}$ in.

182. Blue composition plaque on which is inscribed
. $\frac{3}{4}$ in. × $\frac{5}{8}$ in.

183. Lapis-lazuli scarab inscribed .
Length, $\frac{1}{2}$ in.

184. Brown steatite scarab inscribed 
Length, $\frac{7}{16}$ in.

185. Green glazed steatite scarab inscribed on base 
n(?) *n*(?) *ka.* Length, $\frac{11}{16}$ in.

186. Yellow paste scarab inscribed on base .
Naucratis. Length, $\frac{9}{16}$ in.

187. Green glazed steatite scarab inscribed  . . . .
menχet. Length, $\frac{1}{2}$ in.

188. Stone scarab (broken) inscribed 
Length, $\frac{9}{16}$ in.

189. Yellow glazed steatite scarab inscribed *Hui neb* (?) . . . . . .
Length, $\frac{7}{8}$ in.

190. Yellow glazed scarab inscribed with winged disk, , male figure adoring the god Åmen, ram-headed, and wearing , the crown of Upper and Lower Egypt, *i.e.*, of the North and South ; above is the sign *men.*
Length, $\frac{5}{8}$ in.

191. Dark yellow glazed scarab inscribed with 1, , *ānχ*, on each side of which is an uræus , 2, double *ut'at* , and 3, *Nefer-ka.* Length, $\frac{5}{8}$ in.

192. Purple glazed steatite scarab, inscribed with figures of a deity wearing , Åmen , Rā , and *neb ḥeb mȧ Mentu*, "lord of festivals like Mentu" (Rā).
Length, $\frac{7}{8}$ in.

193. Brownish-yellow glazed steatite scarab inscribed with winged beetle, wearing double plumes and two vultures. Length, $1\frac{1}{4}$ in.

194. Light yellow glazed steatite scarab inscribed the beetle representing the god Cheperȧ, and the two uræi Isis and Nephthys. Length, $\frac{11}{16}$ in.

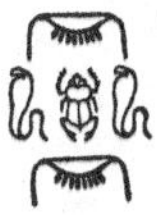

195. Yellow glazed steatite scarab inscribed with *ka net nefer*, surrounded by a spiral ornament.
Length, $\frac{9}{16}$ in.

196. Gray glazed steatite scarab inscribed with and , the emblems of royalty and dominion ; on the upper part are a fish and an ornament composed of triangles and dots. Length, $\frac{9}{16}$ in.

197. Green glazed steatite scarab inscribed 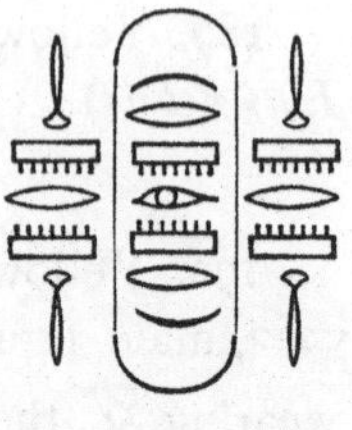

Length, $\frac{11}{16}$ in.

198. Light yellow glazed cowroid inscribed on base with emblems of royalty, 

Length, $\frac{5}{8}$ in.

199. Brown glazed steatite scarab inscribed with plants, double ☥, "life," and a beetle, emblem of Cheperà 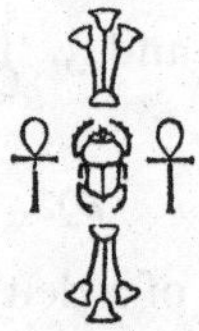

Length, $\frac{9}{16}$ in.

200. Gray glazed steatite scarab inscribed on base  These signs represent "power," "good luck," and "giver of life," or "may he give life."

Length, $\frac{3}{4}$ in.

201. Glazed steatite scarab inscribed 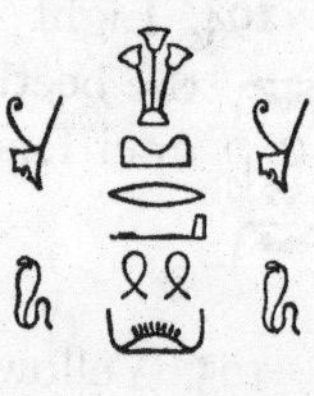

Length, $\frac{3}{4}$ in.

202. Steatite scarab, inscribed with  and ornament composed of  repeated. 

Length, $1\frac{3}{8}$ in.

[1] The broken space represents characters which I cannot read.

203. Green glazed steatite scarab inscribed on base *neter neb taiu,* "god, lord of the two countries."

Length, $1\frac{1}{8}$ in.

204. Yellow glazed steatite oval. Obverse, the goddess *Ta-urt*, and *nefer.* Reverse, *Āmen nebt(?) sānχ-k em nif ānχ.*

Length, $\frac{5}{8}$ in.

205. Glazed yellow faïence scarab inscribed on base *ṭā Rā neb* (?), "a gift of Rā, the lord"!

Length, $\frac{7}{16}$ in.

206. Brown glazed steatite scarab, inscribed . . . *t renpit ḥeḥ Rā Ḥeru,* "[May give] Rā and Horus millions of years of life." Length, $\frac{3}{4}$ in.

207. Dark blue paste scarab inscribed *maāt-en-āb,* "heart of law." Length, $\frac{7}{16}$ in.

208. Brown glazed steatite scarab inscribed, uræus wearing disk, and *Men-nut* (?), "the stablisher of the town" (?), enclosed in a rope border.

Length, $\frac{5}{8}$ in.

209. Gray steatite scarab inscribed with *ut'at*

Length, $\frac{3}{8}$ in.

210. Gray glazed steatite scarab inscribed with double *ut'at*, and diamond ornament. Length, $\frac{5}{8}$ in.

211. Green glazed steatite square plano-convex plaque inscribed with *maāt*, double "Law," *nefer*, "beautiful," and. Length, $\frac{7}{8}$ in.

212. Green glazed steatite scarab, inscribed *nefer*, "good (luck)." Length, $\frac{1}{2}$ in.

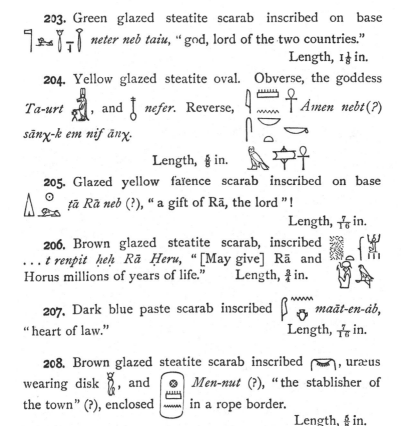

213. Light yellow glazed steatite scarab inscribed *suten ānχ nefer*, "royal, fair life." Length, ½ in.

214. Light green glazed scarab inscribed

Length, $\frac{9}{16}$ in.

215. Gray steatite plaque, on which is inscribed , an obelisk, uræus and lotus flower; on the other side is a fish.

Length, ¾ in.

216. Green glazed faïence plaque, rounded at one end. On one side is inscribed a sphinx and *neb ṭā men*; on the other is a fish. Length, $\frac{13}{16}$ in.

217. Gray glazed steatite plaque in the shape of a tablet . On one side is a cynocephalus ape , on the other winged disk , Rā , Ȧmen , hare , and two illegible signs. Length, ¾ in.

218. Brownish-gray steatite scarab inscribed with ornament composed of lotus buds, double *nefer* , beetle , and two uræi . Length, ¾ in.

219. Light yellow glazed steatite scarab inscribed with *ka*, on each side of which is a hawk ; disk of the sun , on each side of which is an *ut'at* ; beetle , emblem of the god Cheperȧ, on each side of which is *kat*; below is (?). Length, ¾ in.

220. Light gray glazed steatite scarab inscribed with ape, holding *nefer* in his two forepaws, and wearing on his head *maāt*, and an unknown sign. Length, $\frac{11}{16}$ in.

221. Brown glazed steatite cowroid, inscribed with the hieroglyphic signs for "stability," *ṭeṭ*, "life," *ānχ*, "gold," *nub*, and "royalty," *suten*.

Found at Ephesus. Length, ¾ in.

222. Gray glazed steatite scarab inscribed with the figure of a king seated upon a throne, holding in his right hand *ānχ*, and in his left a libation vase ; before him is the sceptre . Length, $\frac{11}{16}$ in.

223. Greenish-brown glazed steatite scarab inscribed with the *uat'* sceptre, ; on one side is a figure wearing , on the other is a figure . Length, $1\frac{3}{16}$ in.

224. Yellow glazed steatite plaque, square, and pierced. Obverse *men neb neb.* Reverse partly effaced. $1\frac{3}{16}$ in. × $1\frac{1}{8}$ in.

225. Light blue glazed steatite scarab inscribed (?) . Length, $1\frac{1}{8}$ in.

226. Green glazed steatite cowroid inscribed with sign for "goddess" or "lord" .

Tell el-Amarna. Length, $\frac{5}{8}$ in.

227. White glazed steatite scarab inscribed *χeper-ta-neferu.* Border, a triple line. Length, $\frac{7}{8}$ in.

228. Whitish-yellow steatite scarab inscribed with figure of Rā (?) wearing disk, and . Length, $\frac{3}{4}$ in.

229. Yellow glazed steatite scarab inscribed with figure of Horus , sphinx , and winged uræus. Length, $\frac{3}{4}$ in.

230. Yellow glazed steatite scarab inscribed with figure of a man on horseback holding the whip and crook ; in the background is the figure of a young man. Length, $\frac{3}{4}$ in.

231. Blue composition scarab inscribed on base *Rā neb.* Length, $\frac{1}{4}$ in.

232. Green glazed steatite scarab inscribed with *ut'at*, *χeper*, and double *ānχ*. Length, $\frac{5}{8}$ in.

233. Yellow glazed steatite scarab inscribed, in outline, with the figure of a man wearing a tunic, *nefer*, "good luck," and *usr*, "power." Length, $1\frac{1}{16}$ in.

234. Grayish-brown steatite scarab inscribed with two uræi and kneeling figure holding a palm branch, emblem of long life, in each hand. Length, $\frac{3}{4}$ in.

235. Green glazed steatite scarab inscribed on base with hieroglyphic characters for "beautiful," *nefer*, "divinity" *ārat*, and "lordship," *neb*. Length, $\frac{5}{8}$ in.

236. Greenish-gray steatite scarab inscribed with gryphon, *ānχ*, "life," *Rā*, "Rā," and *nefer*, "good luck." Length, $\frac{5}{8}$ in.

237. Yellow glazed steatite scarab inscribed and double spiral ornament. Length, $\frac{5}{8}$ in.

238. Green glazed steatite scarab inscribed with figure of Horus, *Ḥeru*, crowns of Upper and Lower Egypt, *seχet*, and *ut'at*. Length, $\frac{9}{16}$ in.

239. Yellow glazed steatite scarab inscribed with *ut'at*, papyrus sceptre, *uat'*, and crown, , written twice. Length, $\frac{7}{16}$ in.

240. Gray glazed steatite scarab inscribed on base with two crocodiles and *neferu*. Length, $1\frac{1}{8}$ in.

241. Dark green stone square plaque, with sphinx, and *ānχ ḥes*. Length, $\frac{3}{4}$ in.

242. Light brown glazed steatite scarab inscribed with sign for "beauty," *nefer*, on each side of which are *ḥā*, two *ut'ats*, sign for life, *ānχ*, and two crowns.

Length, $\frac{3}{4}$ in.

243. White glazed steatite scarab inscribed with obelisk, uræus, and lotus flower. Length, $\frac{5}{8}$ in.

244. Light yellow glazed steatite scarab inscribed with hawk, winged uræus, ape, human figure in adoration, hawk wearing crown, winged uræus, and winged figure.

Length, $\frac{11}{16}$ in.

245. Green glazed Egyptian porcelain scarab inscribed on base *nefer*, and cynocephalus ape. Length, $\frac{7}{16}$ in.

246. Yellow glazed steatite bead, in the shape of three scarabs, on which are inscribed two *ut'ats*, the emblem of "stability," *ṭeṭ*, and double *neb*.

Length, $\frac{9}{16}$ in.

247. Yellow glazed steatite scarab inscribed with cynocephalus ape wearing disk and crescent, and uræus. In front is an obelisk. Length, $\frac{5}{8}$ in.

248. Yellow glazed steatite scarab (broken) inscribed with figure of an animal and *χen* (?) *ḥetep*.

Length, $\frac{9}{16}$ in.

249. Green glazed steatite scarab inscribed *ȧ nefer χen*. Length, $\frac{1}{2}$ in.

250. Yellowish-green glazed faïence scarab with figure of jackal having his head turned behind him, , and (?). Length, $\frac{1}{2}$ in.

251. Green glazed faïence scaraboid (broken) inscribed (?). (?) Length, $\frac{11}{16}$ in.

252. White glazed steatite scarab inscribed with , and seated figure having on its head.

Naucratis. Length, 1/2 in.

253. Dark stone plaque; obverse, figure of a man fighting ; reverse, man seated, before him flowers.

Length, 1 3/16 in.

254. Light yellow glazed steatite scarab inscribed with the figure of a man adoring Rā . Length, 9/16 in.

255. White glazed steatite scarab inscribed *nefer en nefer neb.* Length, 5/8 in.

256. White stone scarab inscribed with a growing plant . Length, 7/8 in.

257. Gray glazed steatite scarab inscribed with the figure of a man holding a flower to his nose, and four rudely made hieroglyphic characters, two of which are *r* and *n*.

Length, 3/4 in.

258. Light yellow glazed steatite animal inscribed with *ānχ*, and an animal. Length, 5/8 in.

259. Light y llow glazed steatite scarab inscribed with sphinx, palm branch, and *ānχ*, life. Length, 3/4 in.

260. Green glazed Egyptian porcelain scarab inscribed *ānχ*, "life." Length, 3/16 in.

261. Gray glazed steatite scarab inscribed with annular ornaments, two uræi, and *ānχ*. Length, 11/16 in.

262. Gray glazed steatite scarab inscribed on base with cynocephalus ape, wearing disk and *ānχ* "life."

Length, 1/2 in.

263. White glazed steatite scarab inscribed with hippopotamus and uræus . Length, 3/4 in.

264. Yellow glazed steatite scarab with hawk-headed lion, uræus , and crocodile . Length, $\frac{15}{16}$ in.

265. Yellow glazed steatite scarab inscribed with uræus  and gryphon. Length, $\frac{3}{4}$ in.

266. Light yellow glazed steatite scarab inscribed 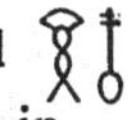 *uaḥ nefer*, and a line ornament. Length, $\frac{3}{4}$ in.

267. Yellow glazed scarab inscribed ..... 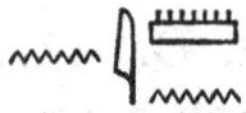 ..... *en Åmen.* Length, $\frac{1}{2}$ in.

268. Square lapis-lazuli plaque inscribed with the figure of a man having both arms raised, and a cartouche in which are inscribed illegible hieroglyphics ; above it is  ?).
Length, $\frac{13}{16}$ in.

269. Lapis-lazuli oval. Obverse, two upright figures. Reverse, . Length, $\frac{3}{4}$ in.

270. Light yellow steatite scarab inscribed with a crocodile  and ram . Length, $\frac{3}{4}$ in.

271. Bluish-gray stone oval, inscribed with vulture .
Length, $\frac{1}{2}$ in.

272. Yellow glazed steatite scarab inscribed with vulture  and  *men.* Length, $\frac{5}{8}$ in.

273. Light yellow glazed steatite scarab inscribed with a lion . Length, $\frac{9}{16}$ in.

274. Brown glazed steatite scarab inscribed .
Length, $\frac{1}{2}$ in.

275. Yellow glazed steatite scarab inscribed with a growing plant . Length, $\frac{5}{8}$ in.

276. Light yellow glazed scarab inscribed with the figure of a man adoring a serpent. Length, $\frac{11}{16}$ in.

277. Green glazed steatite scarab inscribed with a mounted horseman riding over a prostrate foe. Length, $1\frac{1}{4}$ in.

278. Green glazed faïence scarab inscribed with figure of a king seated on a throne. Length, $1\frac{1}{4}$ in.

279. Light gray glazed steatite scarab inscribed with a crocodile(?)-headed god holding a flower and two uræi. Length, $\frac{13}{16}$ in.

280. Gray glazed steatite scarab inscribed with crocodile and a king holding a flower. Length, 1 in.

281. Dark brown glazed steatite scarab inscribed with the figure of a man riding upon a lion, and a boy riding a donkey. Length, $\frac{13}{16}$ in.

282. Green glazed steatite scarab inscribed with ornament formed of lines and lotus buds. Length, $\frac{9}{16}$ in.

283. Brownish-yellow glazed steatite scarab inscribed with line ornament. Length, $\frac{3}{4}$ in.

284. Green glazed porcelain scarab inscribed with a bird (eagle?). Length, $1\frac{1}{8}$ in.

285. Brown glazed steatite scarab inscribed with design composed of leaves and spirals. Length, $1\frac{1}{4}$ in.

286. Green glazed porcelain cowroid inscribed with a design formed of lotus buds. Length, $\frac{5}{8}$ in.

287. Light brown glazed steatite scarab inscribed with a design formed of lotus buds. Length, $\frac{7}{16}$ in.

288. Yellow glazed steatite scarab inscribed with a line ornament. Length, $\frac{3}{4}$ in.

289. White glazed steatite scarab inscribed with spiral ornaments. Length, $\frac{11}{16}$ in.

290. White paste scarab inscribed with winged, bearded lion, standing. Naucratis. Length, $\frac{9}{16}$ in.

291. White glazed steatite scarab inscribed with two uræi. Length, $\frac{7}{16}$ in.

292. Yellow glazed steatite scarab inscribed with two uræi and a hawk (?). Length, $\frac{9}{16}$ in.

293. Blue glazed faïence scarab inscribed with line ornaments. Length. $\frac{9}{16}$ in.

294. Yellow paste scarab inscribed with illegible sign and figure of a bird (?). Naucratis. Length, $\frac{9}{16}$ in.

295. Yellowish-brown glazed steatite scarab inscribed with annular ornaments. Length, $\frac{13}{16}$ in.

296. Sard scarab, uninscribed. Length, 1 in.

297. Green glass scarab, uninscribed. Roman period. Length, $\frac{11}{16}$ in.

298. Grayish-green stone scaraboid, uninscribed. Length, $\frac{7}{16}$ in.

299. Blue glazed faïence scarab, uninscribed. Length, $\frac{3}{8}$ in.

300. Green glazed faïence scarab, uninscribed. Length, $\frac{5}{16}$ in.

301. Cobalt-blue faïence scarab, uninscribed. Length, $\frac{1}{2}$ in.

302. Dark gray stone scarab, uninscribed, from the breast of a mummy. Length, $1\frac{7}{8}$ in.

303. Green basalt scarab, uninscribed, from the breast of a mummy. Thebes. Length, $1\frac{3}{4}$ in.

304. Brown and green glazed steatite scarab inscribed 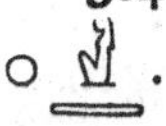. From the hand of the mummy of a female. Length, $\frac{5}{8}$ in.

305. Black obsidian scarab, uninscribed, from the beadwork of a mummy. Aḥmîm (?). Length, $\frac{3}{4}$ in.

306. Blue glazed faïence scarab with outspread wings; from the beadwork covering of a mummy of a late period. The wings are not a pair. Thebes. Width, $5\frac{1}{2}$ in.

307. Blue glazed faïence scarab, with outspread wings; from the beadwork covering of a mummy of a late period. The wings are not a pair. Width, $4\frac{1}{2}$ in.

MISCELLANEOUS OBJECTS IN FAÏENCE, ALABASTER, WOOD, ETC.

308. Painted wooden figure of a hawk  wearing a gilded disk; from the cover of the square cavity in the base of a Ptaḥ-Seker-Ȧusȧr figure, in which the mummified heart of a human being was placed. Aḥmîm. Length, 5 in.

309. Painted wooden human-headed bird , from a corner of the cover of the square cavity in base of a Ptaḥ-Seker-Ȧusȧr figure, in which the mummified heart of a human being was placed. Aḥmîm. Height, 2$\frac{5}{8}$ in.

310. Bronze axe-head  with rounded cutting edge. Thebes. Length, 4$\frac{5}{8}$ in.; width at cutting edge, 3$\frac{1}{4}$ in.; width at end where fastened to blade, 4 in.

311. Pair of ivory hands and arms, ornamented with bracelets and lines, and pierced at one end. Thebes. Length, 7$\frac{1}{8}$ in.

312. Red terra-cotta bowl filled with dried aromatic herbs, from a tomb at Aḥmîm. Diameter, 4$\frac{1}{2}$ in.

313. Fine white marble jar  for holding stibium. 2$\frac{3}{8}$ in. high.

314. Fine alabaster sepulchral jar with square edge. Thebes. 9$\frac{1}{4}$ in. × 4$\frac{5}{8}$ in.

315. Fine alabaster jar with rounded edge. Thebes. 7$\frac{5}{8}$ in. × 4$\frac{3}{4}$ in.

316. Fine alabaster unguent vase with flat projecting rim. Thebes. 8$\frac{1}{2}$ in.

317. Fine alabaster vase with handle . Thebes. 6$\frac{1}{2}$ in. high.

318. Fine alabaster vase with cover. Thebes. 4$\frac{1}{4}$ in.

319. Fine alabaster bowl . Thebes. 7$\frac{1}{2}$ in. diameter.

320. Round alabaster table, placed in the tomb to hold vessels of alabaster filled with unguents, preserves of fruit, etc.
Thebes. 13 in. diameter.

All the above alabaster objects were made from the limestone mountains opposite Thebes.

321. Green and black porphyry *kohl* pot; the stick is wanting. Memphis. $2\frac{5}{8}$ in. high.

322. Dark porphyry vase and cover.
Thebes. 4 in. high.

323. Black diorite bowl .
Thebes. $9\frac{1}{2}$ in. diameter.

324. Black basalt slab and muller for grinding paint.
Thebes. $6\frac{1}{4}$ in. × $3\frac{5}{8}$ in.

325. Painted and glazed red terra-cotta jar, with flat projecting rim inscribed 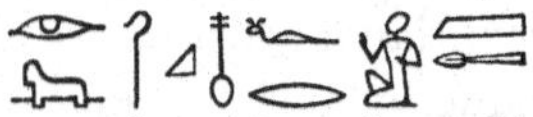 *Ȧusȧr ḥeq nefer maāt*χ*eru*, "Osiris, Ḥeq-nefer, triumphant"!
Thebes, XXth dynasty, about B.C. 1200. Height, $5\frac{3}{4}$ in.

326. Flat, rounded, calcareous stone box, the cover of which is painted blue and yellow. The two parts of the box have square, pierced projections, and were fastened together by wooden pegs driven through them; the cover is inscribed  *Ȧusȧr ḥeq-nefer maāt-*χ*eru*, "Osiris, Ḥeq-nefer, triumphant"!
Thebes, XXth dynasty, about B.C. 1200. Diameter, $3\frac{7}{8}$ in.

327. Bronze vessel with handle, four feet, and flat projecting rim.
Aḥmîm, Arabic period. Depth, $2\frac{5}{8}$ in.; diameter, 5 in.

328. Oval bronze mirror, gilded on one side. It was originally fixed in a wooden handle, which fell to pieces on exposure to the air. From a tomb of the XXVIth dynasty, about B.C. 550.
Thebes. Greatest diameter, $7\frac{7}{16}$ in.; least diameter, 7 in.

329. Bronze figure of the god Harpocrates ( *Ḥeru p* χ*raṭ*, *i.e.*, "Horus the child") wearing disk, plumes

, uræus 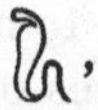, and curl on the right side of his head. The eyes are inlaid with gold. The base is inscribed :—

Ḥeru p χraṭ ur ḥetep en Åmen ṭā ānχ χensu
Harpocrates, mighty one first of Åmen, giver of life, Chonsu-

Peṭā - res se T'eṭ-ḥrå mes neb pa Nesi - Ḥeru
Peta - res, son of T'eṭ-hra, born of the lady of the house, Nesi - Horus.

That is to say, it was dedicated to Harpocrates by Chonsu-Petā-res, grand-son of Nesi-Horus. This figure is a piece of very fine Egyptian bronze work, and is a good example of the best productions of this class during the XIXth or XXth dynasty. Thebes. Height, 6¼ in.

330. Bronze figure of Isis suckling Horus. She wears horns, disk, and uræus on her head.
Ptolemaic period, about B.C. 200.
Presented by J. W. Clark, M.A.

331. Four pieces of blue and yellow glazed faïence bead work. The beads were found in the coffins of the Middle Empire, and have been re-strung on modern thread by modern Egyptian women. Thebes.

332. Strings of blue, white, and red glazed faïence bead-work re-strung on modern thread. The small, rudely made, uninscribed *ushabtiu* figures tied to them are of a much later period. Thebes.

333. String of blue, green, red, and yellow faïence flat beads, some with serrated edges. Thebes. Length, 12½ in.

334. Necklace of light green and dark blue glazed faïence beads. Thebes.

335. White glazed faïence draughtsman. Height, 1 in.

336. Fragment of a green glazed faïence model of a boomerang, inscribed with the prenomen of Thothmes III., *Rā-men-χeper*, and ornamented with on each side. Thebes. Length, 6 in.

337. Green glazed rectangular faïence pendant, pierced with figures of four deities, in hollow-work.
Length, $1\frac{1}{2}$ in. × $1\frac{1}{4}$ in.
Presented by Prof. W. Robertson Smith.

338. Blue glazed faïence model of a fruit. Length, 1 in.

339. White glazed faïence ring. Diameter, $\frac{7}{8}$ in.

340. Blue glazed faïence ring. Diameter, $\frac{13}{16}$ in.

341. Fragment of blue glazed faïence ring.
Diameter, $\frac{5}{8}$ in.

342. Green glazed faïence ring with bezel, in the shape of head of Hathor. Diameter, $\frac{7}{8}$ in.

343. Blue glazed faïence ring with bezel, inscribed with the name of Åmen-Rā, . Diameter, $\frac{7}{8}$ in.

344. Three white and green glazed faïence *ut'ats* .
Length, $\frac{3}{8}$ in.

345. Green glazed faïence . Length, $\frac{13}{16}$ in.

346. Four green glazed faïence *uat'* sceptres .
Lengths, $2\frac{1}{4}$, 2, $1\frac{7}{8}$, and 1 in.

347. Blue glazed faïence uræus . Height, $\frac{1}{2}$ in.

348. Circular, flat glazed faïence bead, on one side of which is a line device.

349. Green glazed faïence leaf-shaped pendant.
Length, $1\frac{3}{4}$ in.

350. Green glazed faïence *ṭeṭ* . Height, $\frac{7}{8}$ in.

351. Green glazed faïence figure of Harpocrates.
Length, $1\frac{3}{4}$ in.

352. Green glazed faïence figure of Isis suckling Horus. Length, 1⅞ in.

353. Green glazed faïence figure of Chnemu, ram-headed. Height, 1⅝ in.

354. Green glazed faïence figure of Ptaḥ-Seker-Osiris. Height, 1¼ in.

Presented by Prof. W. Robertson Smith.

355. Green and black glazed faïence pendent figure of Thoth, , ibis-headed, on the base of which is inscribed  "Lord of Chemennu. . . ." Height, ¾ in.

356. Green glazed faïence pendent hare , emblem of Osiris. Length, 1 in.

357. Dark blue glazed faïence figure of Qebḥsennuf, from the beadwork of a mummy. Height, 3⅛ in.

358. Blue glazed, black striped faïence figure of Ḥāpi, from the beadwork of a mummy. Height, 2½ in.

359. Fragment of a linen bandage from a mummy, inscribed in hieratic with parts of the 113th and 114th chapters of the Book of the Dead. These chapters are entitled respectively , "The Chapter of knowing the spirits of Chen," and  , "The Chapter of knowing the spirits of Chemennu." For the hieroglyphic text, see Lepsius, *Todtenbuch*, Bl. XLIII., and Naville, *Das Aegyptische Todtenbuch*, Bl. CXXV.; for translations, see Birch in Bunsen's *Egypt's Place in Universal History*, Vol. V., pp. 246, 247, and Pierret, *Le Livre des Morts*, p. 341 ff. This fragment belongs to a mummy of a late period, and was probably inscribed about B.C. 300. Length, 8½ in. × 3½ in.

360. Flat, cylindrical paste bead, inscribed on one side 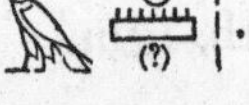. Diameter, ½ in.

361. Yellow steatite figure of the god Bes wearing plumes. Height, 1 in.

362. Blue glazed paste bead, inscribed . Length, $\frac{9}{16}$ in.

363. Green glazed faïence bead, obverse , reverse , scorpion. Length, $\frac{7}{16}$ in.

364. Yellow steatite figure of the god Shu with hands raised, supporting the disk of the sun. Height, $1\frac{1}{8}$ in.

365. Flat cylindrical paste bead inscribed on one side *χeperà neb taui*, "Cheperà, lord of the two worlds."
Nos. 360–365 are from Naucratis. Diameter, $\frac{1}{2}$ in.

366. Green stone pendent figure of the god Thoueris. Height, $2\frac{1}{2}$ in.

Presented by Prof. W. Robertson Smith.

367. Wax figure of Ḥāpi. Height, $2\frac{3}{4}$ in.

368. Red glass split ring. Diameter, $\frac{1}{2}$ in.

369. Red jasper buckle . Length, 1 in.

370. Black stone plumes . Length, $1\frac{3}{8}$ in.

371. Mummied snake.

372. Part of an arrow in the head of which is a flat flint, fastened by being inserted in a slit, and bound round with gummed linen. Thebes. Length, $8\frac{3}{4}$ in.

373. Necklace of carnelian, and blue, yellow, and white glazed faïence beads, strung on modern thread. Thebes. Length, $9\frac{7}{8}$ in.

374. Fragment of plaster hand from a coffin, on one of the fingers of which is an imitation ring. Part of the mummy cloth to which it was fastened still adheres to it. Thebes. Roman period.

375. Upper part of bronze figure of Osiris, wearing crown and plumes, and holding and in his hands, which are crossed over the breast. Height, 5½ in.

376. Pendent bronze figure of Osiris, as above; the pedestal on which it stood is wanting.
Roman period. Height, 3½ in.

377. Bronze figure of Osiris, as above.
Roman period. Height, 3¼ in.

378. Bronze figure of the god Bes, wearing plumes, with right hand raised. Pedestal wanting.
Roman period. Height, 2⅞ in.

379. Bronze kneeling figure of a man with both hands raised in adoration. XXVIth dynasty. Height, 1¾ in.

380. Bronze figure of the hawk of Horus .
Height, 2 in.

381. Bronze head and neck of ibis, , sacred to Thoth.
Height, 1¾ in.

382. Green glazed porcelain pendent plaque with *ut'at*, , in relief. 1¼ in. × 1 in.

383. Green glazed porcelain pendent plaque with *ut'at* , in hollow-work. ⅝ in.

384. Bronze uræus inlaid with lapis-lazuli and carnelian from the head of a statue. 1¼ in.

Nos. 382–384 *were presented by H. H. Harrod, Esq., of Peterhouse.*

385. Two wooden pillows which were buried with mummies in a tomb. Thebes. Height, 9 in. and 8¼ in.

386. Gray granite *ut'at* . Naucratis. Length, 1⅛ in.

387. Bone pendant, on one side of which is a Coptic saint on horseback spearing a dragon (?). Length, 2¾ in.

388. Terra-cotta vase, the opening of which has been closed by linen and bitumen. Outside, at nearly equal intervals, are three impressions of a scarab ; inside are three fruits. Height, 3¾ in.

389. Roughly made sycamore wood model of a coffin containing a wooden *ushabti* figure made for 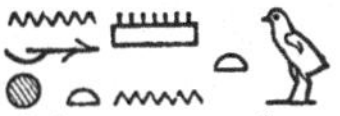 Neχt-Mentu, and inscribed in hieroglyphics with a version of the 6th chapter of the Book of the Dead.

Thebes. Length of coffin, 11½ in.; height of figure, 8 in.

390. Limestone altar with rectangular hollow, on which are inscribed representations of a number of offerings, fruit, flowers, meat, cakes, etc., made for 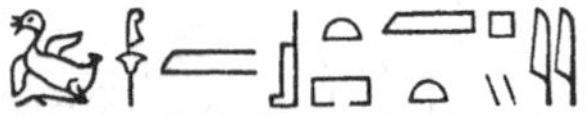  *t'a em àuset maāt Pepia*, " Pepia, the flabellum bearer in the seat of law." The flat raised edge is inscribed with two lines of hieroglyphics which contain the usual prayers to Osiris, Anubis, Hathor, and Maāt; on the front edge are three lines which read from the middle to the right and left respectively, and on the side edges and the rounded back edge are two lines. The characters are very rudely cut, and the many breaks in the lines make it difficult to give a connected text. On the right hand, at the top, the prenomen and name of Amenophis I., and the name of Àḥmes-nefert-àri, are mentioned.

Suten	Ser-ka-Rā	maātχeru	se Rā	Àmen-ḥetep
King	*Ser-ka-Rā,*	*triumphant,*	*son of the sun,*	*Àmenḥetep,*

maātχeru	neter ḥemt	Àāḥ-mes-nefer-àri	maātχeru
triumphant,	*divine spouse,*	*Àḥmes-nefert-àri,*	*triumphant.*

The inscriptions on the sides mention the names of his sons and daughters.

Early XVIIIth dynasty. 18½ in. × 12¾ in.

391. Sandstone fragment of irregular shape, inscribed with the fragments of five lines of hieroglyphics, which contain the following cartouches :—

. . . . *se Rā Ȧmen meri Uasȧrken* (*I.*).

. . . *Usr-maāt Rā setep Ȧmen se Rā Ȧmen-meri Śaśanq* (*III.*).

Usr-maāt-Rā setep Ȧmen se-Rā Ȧmen-meri Uasȧrken (*II.*).

14½ in. × 8½ in.

392. Fragment of sandstone stele, of irregular shape, inscribed with the fragments of six mutilated lines of hieroglyphics; it appears to have been written for a scribe, and set up in the "sixth day of the first month of the season of inundation in the eighteenth year of the reign of Osorkon II. or Shashanq III." 

12 in. × 10½ in.

393. Black basalt base of a statue of Psammetichus, of which nothing but parts of the feet remain. This dignitary lived during the reign of Amāsis II., king of Egypt, about B.C. 550. It was found among the ruins of Saïs by Dr. E. D. Clarke,[1] and was presented by him to the Fitzwilliam Museum, Cambridge.

[1] This inscription was published by E. D. Clarke, in his *Travels in various Countries of Europe and Asia*, 3 pts. (printed at Cambridge, Broxbourne, and London respectively), 6 vols., 1810–1823, 4to., vol. 3, p. 218. He also gave an account of it before the Society of Antiquaries, together with a statement of some remarkable views about the meaning of the hieroglyphics. In modern times it has been published, with interlinear translation and transliteration by Prof. Alex. Macalister, in *Proc. Soc. Bibl. Arch.*, 1887, pp. 98–100.

1. 

suten ḥetep ṭā neter āa åmtu ḥet

A royal offering may give the god great within the temple of Neith!

ḥetep ṭā neteru nebu Åmenta ḥetep

An offering may give the gods all of the underworld! May an offering

2. 

ṭā perχeru ta åḥ åpt nef åp

be given, sacrificial meals, cakes, oxen, ducks, to him at the beginning

renpit tep renpit uaḳ mā

of the year, at the festival of the new year, { *at the Uaḳa festival, a sacrificial gift* }

Teḥuti seker ḥeb ur

at the festival of Thoth, at the Seker festival, at the great festival,

3. 

perχeru åp reu ḥet

sepulchral meals at the festival of opening the doors of the temple of Neith,

mā neteru per perχeru

a sacrificial gift { *at the festival of the coming forth of the two gods,* } *sepulchral meals*

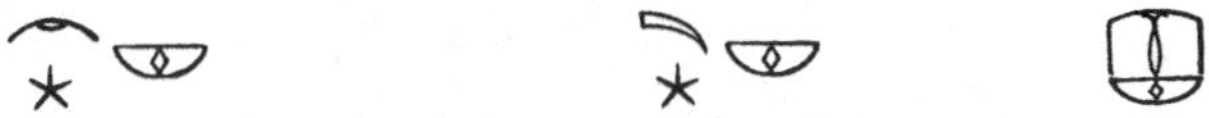

åbeṭ smat ḥeb

at the festival of the month, at the festival of half month, at festival

4. 

neb hru neb t'etta em neb åmaχ

every, on day every, for ever, lord of watchful devotion to

[1] For the festivals see Brugsch, *Thesaurus Inscriptionum Ægyptiacarum*, page 242.

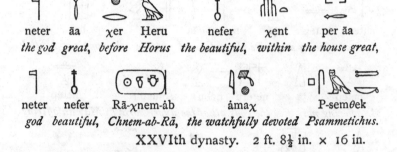

neter āa χer Ḥeru nefer χent per āa
the god great, before Horus the beautiful, within the house great,

neter nefer Rā-χnem-âb âmaχ P-semθek
god beautiful, Chnem-ab-Rā, the watchfully devoted Psammetichus.

XXVIth dynasty. 2 ft. 8½ in. × 16 in.

394. Part of a black basalt statue of Psammetichus II., King of Egypt, about B.C. 596. On the band of his garment, in front, is inscribed   *neter nefer Nefer-âb-Rā se Rā Psemθek Rā mâ*, "Beautiful god, Nefer-âb-Rā, son of the sun, Psammetichus, like the sun." On the square column, at the back, are inscribed the "banner name" and titles of this king :—*menχ* (?) *âb suten net . . . . us.*

XXVIth dynasty. Height, 20½ in.

395. Black basalt head and shoulders of a seated statue, upon which is inscribed 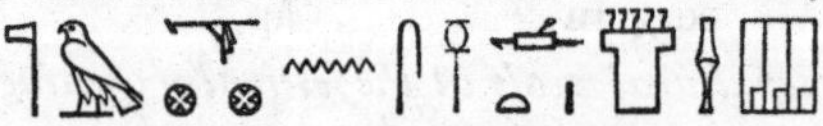 .

XXVIth dynasty. Height, 14in.

396. Sandstone fragment from a Ptolemaic temple, inscribed in relief :—

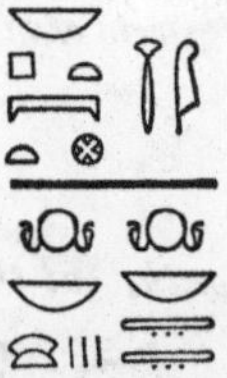

20½ in. × 21 in.

The following objects were presented to the Fitzwilliam Museum by the late Rev. Greville J. Chester, B.A. (Oxon.) :—

397. Mummied cat, seated.

Beni Hasân. XXVIth dynasty. Height, 9½ in.

398. Brown and gray porphyry pot for *kohl*.
Thebes. Height, $\frac{7}{8}$ in.

399. Bronze case for holding small mummied serpent.
Lower Egypt. $2\frac{1}{4}$ in. × $1\frac{1}{16}$ in. × $\frac{7}{8}$ in.

400. Bronze spear head. Ḳurnah. $3\frac{5}{8}$ in.

401. Two bronze fragments of some instrument.
Thebes.

402. Hæmatite weight. Karnak. $1\frac{3}{8}$ in.

403. Thirteen glazed faïence roundels, ornamented with rosettes, for inlaying in walls.
From the palace of Rameses II. at Tell el-Yahûdîyyêh.

404. Glazed faïence paint holder, with two holes, in the form of a cartouche 𓍷. Ṣaḳḳârah. Length, $2\frac{3}{8}$ in

405. Square calcareous stone mould for making figures of the *bennu* bird 𓅣. $3\frac{1}{2}$ in.

406. Red terra-cotta vase. Gîzeh. $2\frac{1}{8}$ in. high.

407. Glazed faïence vase. Ṣaḳḳârah. 2 in. high.

408. Cobalt-blue glazed faïence fragment, with annular ornament. Tell el-Amarna. $2\frac{1}{2}$ in. × $1\frac{3}{8}$ in.

409. Green glazed faïence draughtsman.
Thebes. Height, $\frac{3}{4}$ in.

410. Green stone object (disk of sun?).
Thebes. Diameter, $\frac{3}{4}$ in.

411. Fourteen blue, green, yellow, and red glazed faïence pendants, fruits, &c. Tell el-Amarna.

412. Blue glazed faïence left eye 𓁹.
Tell el-Amarna. Length, $1\frac{1}{2}$ in.

413. Blue glazed faïence pendent Hathor head.
Tell el-Amarna. Length, $\frac{1}{2}$ in.

414. Green glazed faïence *ut'at* 𓂀.
Tell el-Amarna. Length, $\frac{5}{8}$ in.

415. Five blue glazed faïence scarabs, uninscribed.
Tell el-Amarna. Length, $\frac{5}{16}$ in. to $\frac{7}{16}$ in.

416. Blue glazed faïence scarab, inscribed ☥ *ānχ*.
Tell el-Amarna. Length, $\frac{3}{8}$ in.

417. Blue glazed faïence bezel of a ring, inscribed

Tell el-Amarna. Length, $\frac{3}{4}$ in.

418. Fruit of the dûm palm, placed with a mummy in a tomb. Length, 2 in.

419. Three imitation dates, placed with a mummy in a tomb. Ḳurnah.

420. Red terra-cotta mould for making faïence models of bunches of grapes. Tell el-Amarna. $1\frac{7}{8}$ in.

421. Leather shoe for right foot.
Thebes. Length, $7\frac{1}{4}$ in.

422. Three shell split rings ◯. Thebes, $1\frac{1}{8}$, $1\frac{1}{16}$, $\frac{5}{8}$ in.

423. Two carnelian split rings. Thebes, $\frac{1}{2}$, $\frac{7}{16}$ in.

424. Phœnician glass bottle. Aḥmîm. Height, $2\frac{7}{8}$ in.

425. Red terra-cotta ostrakon, inscribed with seven lines of Greek Karnak. $5\frac{1}{8}$ in.

426. Red terra-cotta ostrakon, inscribed with four lines of Demotic. Karnak. $4\frac{3}{4}$ in.

427. Red terra-cotta ostrakon, inscribed with three lines of Demotic. Karnak. $3\frac{1}{4}$ in.

428. Red terra-cotta ostrakon, inscribed with five lines of Coptic. Karnak. $3\frac{3}{4}$ in.

ⲗⲉⲗⲟⲩ ▒▒▒ ⲙⲟⲛⲥⲏ ▒▒▒
ⲡⲉⲧⲉⲙⲙⲉⲛⲱⲫⲓⲙⲙⲓⲩⲥⲓ
ⲥⲩⲣⲟⲥⲗⲉⲗⲟⲩⲧⲟⲩ (?) ▒▒▒
ⲡⲓϫⲉ ⲓⲥ ⲡ (?) ⲁ (?) ⲛⲁⲙⲉⲟⲩ
ⲗⲉⲗⲟⲩ ▒▒▒

429. Iron key with fragment of linen cord attached.
Thebes. Length, 5 in.

430. Bronze key. Thebes. Length, $1\frac{7}{8}$ in.

431. Grotesque terra-cotta head.
Menshîyeh. Length, $\frac{5}{8}$ in.

432. Upper part of terra-cotta figure of a female.
Fayyûm. Height, $2\frac{5}{8}$ in.

433. Bronze key ring. Diameter, $\frac{3}{4}$ in.

434. Pendent bronze Coptic cross.
Abûṣîr, near Ṣaḳḳârah. Length, $1\frac{1}{4}$ in.

435. Bronze Coptic lamp, with cross on the handle, and cover in the form of a shell. Length, $3\frac{3}{8}$ in.

436. Glass Coptic cross. Medinet Habû. Length, $\frac{3}{4}$ in.

437. Glass Thoueris. Aḫmîm. Height, 1 in.

438. Two glass roundels for inlaying. Arabic period.
Aḫmîm. Diameter, $\frac{1}{2}$ in.

439. Black glass bracelet. Arabic period.
Upper Egypt. Diameter, $3\frac{1}{8}$ in.

440. Black glass bracelet. Arabic period.
Upper Egypt. Diameter, $2\frac{5}{8}$ in.

441. Five fragments of variegated glass beads. Aḫmîm.

442. Fragment of Egyptian fishing net. Aḫmîm.

443. Red terra-cotta vase, in the shape of a pomegranate. To fill this vessel it was necessary to invert it, and to pour the liquid down the funnel which runs into its interior. On the side is a grotesque mask, the mouth of which forms the opening through which the liquid was poured out.
Height, 4 in.

444. Red terra-cotta two-handled bottle, neck wanting, on one side of which is a figure of Mâr Mênas and two camels' heads; on the other side is a cross, etc.
Alexandria. Height, $2\frac{5}{8}$ in.

445. Yellow terra-cotta two-handled bottle, on one side of which is a figure of Mâr Mênas and two camels' heads; on the other, enclosed in a palm-leaf border, is inscribed **ΑΓΙΟΥ ΜΗΝΑ ΕΥΛΟΓ.** Alexandria. Height, $3\frac{1}{4}$ in.

446. Light terra-cotta two-handled bottle, on one side of which is a figure of Mâr Mênas and two camels' heads; on the other, enclosed in a palm-leaf border, is inscribed **ΕΥΛΟΓΙΑ ΤΟΥ ΑΓΙΟΥ ΜΗΝΑC.**

Alexandria. Height, $3\frac{1}{2}$ in.

447. Green glazed porcelain bead inscribed 𓂀 𓋹 𓂀 𓋹.
Green glazed porcelain bead hollow worked.

448. String of fifteen amber beads.

449. String of carnelian and amethyst beads.

450. String of carnelian beads. Abydos.

451. String of carnelian beads. Aḥmîm.

452. String of hæmatite beads.

453. Necklace of black terra-cotta, and green and red glazed porcelain beads.

454. Necklace of small blue and black glass beads.

455. Six strings of green and yellow, blue and yellow glass, garnet, black clay, and other beads.

456. String of amulets, consisting of mother-of-emerald, carnelian, and faïence figures of Horus, carnelian 𓂀, steatite 𓂀, and faïence figures of gods.

457. Yellow glazed steatite scarab, inscribed on base

se Rā Āpep ānχ sa. $\frac{5}{8}$ in.

458. Blue glazed faïence cowroid inscribed on base 𓄤 *nefer* "good luck." $\frac{1}{2}$ in.

459. Thirty-three glazed faïence beads, bezels of rings, disks, fruits, etc, etc., in green, blue, violet, yellow, and red glazed faïence. Tell el-Amarna.

460. Fragment of alabaster, inscribed  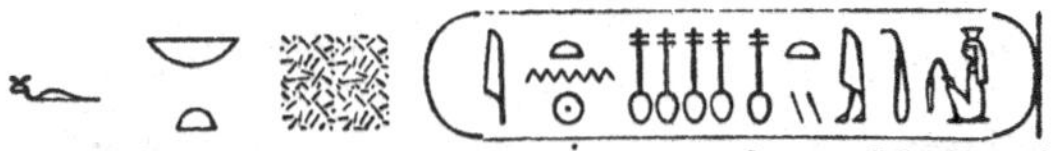 *suten ḥemt urt mert-f neb* . . . . *Āten neferu Nefert-ith*, "Royal wife, mighty lady, loving him, the lady of . . . . Nefert-ith, the beauties of the disk." Nefert-ith was the wife of Amenophis IV., King of Egypt, B.C. 1500. $4\frac{1}{2}$ in. × $3\frac{1}{2}$ in.

461. Three bronze plates from a coat of armour.
Length, $1\frac{3}{4}$ in.

462. Portion of an arrow with flint head. Length, 9 in.

463. Blue and white glass heart, fragment of a ring, flower, and oval object. From Tell el-Amarna.

464. Wooden ring from a mummy. Diameter, $1\frac{5}{8}$ in.

465. Two stone objects in the shape of almonds.
Length, $1\frac{1}{2}$ in.

466. Wooden object in the shape of the beak of a duck(?).
Length, $3\frac{1}{4}$ in.

467. Wooden model of a date. Length, 2 in.

468. Alabaster peg (?). Length, $2\frac{1}{4}$ in.

469. Hæmatite pillow, uninscribed. Length, $1\frac{1}{2}$ in.

470. Hæmatite . Length, $1\frac{1}{8}$ in.

471. Stone heart. Length, $1\frac{1}{4}$ in.

472. Stone *menāt*. Length, $1\frac{1}{4}$ in.

473. Basalt fingers. Length, $3\frac{3}{4}$ in.

474. Gray granite *ut'at*, pierced, to be worn as a pendant.
Length, $1\frac{3}{8}$ in.

475. Three stone and shell split rings.
Diameters, $1\frac{1}{4}$ in., $\frac{7}{8}$ in., $\frac{1}{2}$ in.

476. Three red glass objects. Diameters, $\frac{7}{8}$ in., $\frac{7}{8}$ in., $\frac{5}{8}$ in.

477. Stone . Length, $1\frac{3}{8}$ in.

478. Stone fingers. Length, 1 in.

479. Steatite Thoueris. Length, $\frac{5}{8}$ in.

480. Carnelian Thoueris. Length, $\frac{3}{4}$ in.

481. Fragment of painted *cartonnage* of a mummy, Anubis seated on a tomb . Length, 1$\frac{3}{4}$ in. × $\frac{1}{2}$ in.

482. Steatite stamp, on base two crocodiles . Diameter, $\frac{1}{2}$ in.

483. Bronze spatula. Tell el-Amarna. Length, 4$\frac{3}{4}$ in.

484. Upper part of pendent male figure. Length, 1$\frac{1}{8}$ in.

485. Clay seal from a roll of papyrus. Diameter, 1 in.

486. Black basalt rectangular slab and muller for grinding paint; the hollow in the slab is in the form of a cartouche. 3$\frac{3}{4}$in. × 2$\frac{5}{8}$ in.

487. Rectangular stone slab for grinding paint. 1$\frac{3}{4}$ in. × 1$\frac{1}{8}$ in.

488. Veined marble jar. From Abydos. Height, 2$\frac{1}{4}$ in.

489. Alabaster jar with two handles. From Abydos. Height, 2$\frac{5}{8}$ in.

490. Black basalt jar with two handles. From Abydos. Height, 2$\frac{5}{8}$ in.

491. Diorite jar for holding stibium. Height, 1$\frac{3}{4}$ in.

492. Blackish-green, glazed faïence jar for holding stibium. Height, 2$\frac{1}{8}$ in.

493. White calcareous stone head of a spindle. Tell el-Amarna. Diameter, 2$\frac{3}{4}$ in.

494. White calcareous stone mould for making faïence figures of the god Mesthȧ or Ȧmset. 3$\frac{3}{4}$ in. × 1$\frac{1}{2}$ in.

495. White calcareous stone mould for making faïence figures of a bird. 2 in. × 2 in.

496. Red terra-cotta mould for making faïence figures of the god Bes. 2$\frac{7}{8}$ in. × 2 in.

497. Red terra-cotta mould for making faïence figures of the god Bes. Length, 1 in.

498. Red terra-cotta mould for making faïence figures of a seated deity. Length, 1 in.

499. Red terra-cotta mould for making faïence figures of a god. Length, 2⅛ in.

500. Red terra-cotta mould for making faïence figures of . 1⅝ in. × 1⅜ in.

501. Red terra-cotta mould for making faïence figures of the god Sebek. Length, 1⅜ in.

502. Red terra-cotta mould for making a bunch of grapes. Length, 1¼ in.

503. Red terra-cotta mould for a bezel of a ring, inscribed with a lotus flower and two buds. Length, 1⅜ in.

504. Red terra-cotta mould for the bezel of a ring 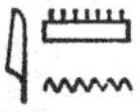 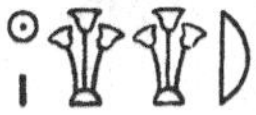. Length, 1⅛ in.

505. Red terra-cotta mould for a semicircular object. 1¾ in. × 1⅝ in.

506-515. Ten Greek ostraka.

516, 517. Two Demotic ostraka.

518. Three fragments of Egyptian glass vases, two glass pendants, a glass bead, circular glass object, and part of brown and white glass jar (?).

519. Red terra-cotta reel painted black. Length, 2⅜ in.

520. Rectangular wooden stamp, inscribed ΛΥ. 2¼ in. × 1⅜ in.

521. Circular wooden stamp, inscribed BOYLIΓE. Diameter, 2⅜ in.

522. Bronze pin, one end in the shape of a spoon. Length, 4½ in.

523. Stone pin, one end in the shape of a spoon. Length, 4¾ in.

524. Wooden tablet, inscribed in Greek and Demotic, for attaching to a mummy. Length, 3 in.

525. Reed or papyrus sandal. Length, $12\frac{1}{2}$ in.

526. Red terra-cotta saucer, painted with three fishes. Diameter, $7\frac{3}{4}$ in.

527. Two terra-cotta saucers. Diameter, $2\frac{1}{2}$ in.

528. Terra-cotta painted vase, with two handles. Height, $2\frac{1}{2}$ in.

529. Terra-cotta lamp, the upper part in the shape of a frog. Length, 3 in.

530. Fragment of a blue glazed faïence head-dress. Length, $3\frac{1}{2}$ in.

531. Cobalt-blue glazed fragment, with annular ornaments. $2\frac{1}{4}$ in. × 2 in.

532. Green glazed faïence *ut'at.* Length, $1\frac{7}{8}$ in.

533. Green glazed faïence *ut'at.* Length, $1\frac{5}{8}$ in.

534. Green glazed faïence papyrus sceptre. Length, $2\frac{1}{8}$ in.

535. Green glazed faïence papyrus sceptre. Length, $1\frac{3}{4}$ in.

536. Green glazed faïence Thoth. Length, $1\frac{5}{8}$ in.

537. Green glazed faïence Anubis. Length, $1\frac{1}{4}$ in.

538, 539. Two green glazed figures of Bes. Length, $\frac{1}{2}$ in.

540. Green glazed faïence uræus. Length, $1\frac{1}{4}$ in.

541. Green glazed faïence Shu. Length, $1\frac{1}{4}$ in.

542. Green glazed faïence buckle . Length, $1\frac{3}{8}$ in.

543. Green glazed faïence buckle . Length, $\frac{3}{4}$ in.

544. Green glazed faïence *teshert* crown . Length, $\frac{7}{8}$ in.

545. Green glazed faïence figure of a woman seated. Length, $\frac{7}{8}$ in.

546. Blue glazed faïence bezel of ring inscribed . Length, $\frac{5}{8}$ in.

547. Blue glazed faïence bezel of ring inscribed  *Rā ḥeḥ nub.* Tell el-Amarna. Length, $\frac{3}{4}$ in.

548. Blue glazed faïence bezel of a ring inscribed  *Rā-χeperu-neb.* Tell el-Amarna. Length, $\frac{3}{4}$ in.

549. Blue glazed faïence fruit. Length, $\frac{7}{8}$ in.

550. Cobalt-blue glazed faïence bezel of ring, inscribed  *Rā-ānχ-χeperu.* Length, $\frac{3}{4}$ in.

551. Green basalt pendant in the shape of a bird. From Abydos. $3\frac{1}{2}$ in. × 3 in.

552. Green basalt pendant in the shape of a fish. From Meshaieh. $4\frac{3}{4}$ in. × $2\frac{7}{8}$ in.

553. Green basalt pendant, in the shape of a sheep (?). From Abydos. $5\frac{1}{4}$ in. × 4 in.

554. Green basalt diamond-shaped object. From Abydos. $10\frac{3}{4}$ in. × $3\frac{3}{4}$ in.

555. Light blue glazed faïence *ushabti* figure made for Pa-ṭā-meḥtet, a divine father of Åmen-Rā. The inscription reads: 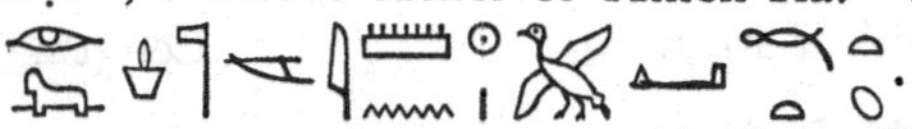. Abydos. Height, $4\frac{3}{4}$ in.

556. Green glazed faïence *ushabti* figure for 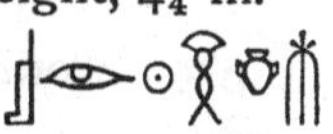  (?) *Åusår Uaḥ-åb-Rā mes en Nes-nub-θeθ* (?), "Osiris, Uaḥ-åb-Rā, born of Nes-nub-theth" (?). Height, $6\frac{1}{4}$ in.

557. Green glazed faïence *ushabti* figure for Amāsis, son of Ḥetep-Bast. The inscription reads:  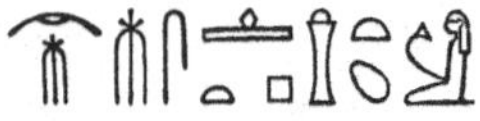. Height, $4\frac{1}{2}$ in.

558, 559. Two blue glazed faïence *ushabtiu* figures, uninscribed. From Abydos. Height, 5 in.

560. Green glazed faïence *ushabti* figure, uninscribed. Height, $2\frac{1}{2}$ in.

561. Wooden *ushabti* figure, inscribed 
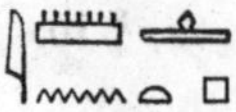. "Osiris, priest of Mut, Åmen-ḥetep." Height, $7\frac{1}{2}$ in.

562. Wooden *ushabti* figure, uninscribed. Height, 5 in.

563. Wooden *ushabti* figure. Late Roman period (?). Height, $6\frac{1}{4}$ in.

564. Bone covering for the corner of a box, with leaves and fruit in relief. Græco-Roman period. Height, $3\frac{1}{8}$ in.

565. Bone doll (?). Height, $2\frac{7}{8}$ in.

566. Two bone spindle heads with annular ornaments. Diameter, 1 in. and $\frac{7}{8}$ in.

567. Bone spindle head. Diameter, $\frac{5}{8}$ in.

568. Bone spindle head, inlaid in red with figures of birds on the wing. Diameter, $\frac{3}{4}$ in.

569. Wooden spindle head with annular ornaments. Diameter, $1\frac{1}{8}$ in.

570. Bronze tweezers for the hair. Length, $2\frac{3}{4}$ in.

571. Bronze tweezers for the hair. Length, $1\frac{5}{8}$ in.

572. Bronze *kohl* stick. Length, $6\frac{1}{2}$ in.

573. Bronze *kohl* stick. Length, 6 in.

574. Bronze *kohl* stick. Length, 5 in.

575. Bronze pin (?). Length, $4\frac{3}{4}$ in.

576. Bronze needle. Length, $4\frac{1}{2}$ in.

577. Bronze bodkin. Length, $6\frac{1}{4}$ in.

INDEX.

The main references are printed in blacker type.

CAMBRIDGE: PRINTED BY C. J. CLAY, M.A. AND SONS, AT THE UNIVERSITY PRESS.

Printed in the United States
By Bookmasters